The Inspiration of Hope
in Bereavement Counselling

of related interest

Spirituality and Mental Health Care
Rediscovering a 'Forgotten' Dimension
John Swinton
ISBN 1 85302 804 5

Grief and Powerlessness
Helping People Regain Control of Their Lives
Ruth Bright
ISBN 1 85302 447 3

Finding a Way Through When Someone Close has Died
What it Feels Like and What You Can Do to Help Yourself:
A Workbook by Young People for Young People
Pat Mood and Lesley Whittaker
ISBN 1 85302 920 3

Spiritual Dimensions of Pastoral Care
Practical Theology in a Multidisciplinary Context
Edited by David Williows and John Swinton
ISBN 1 85302 892 4

Being Mindful, Easing Suffering
Reflections on Palliative Care
Christopher Johns
ISBN 1 84310 212 9

Journeys into Palliative Care
Roots and Reflections
Edited by Christina Mason
ISBN 1 84310 030 4

Suicide
The Tragedy of Hopelessness
David Aldridge
ISBN 1 85302 444 9

The Inspiration of Hope
in Bereavement Counselling

John R. Cutcliffe

Foreword by Ronna Jevne

Jessica Kingsley Publishers
London and Philadelphia

Cover photograph reproduced by permission of Professor Ronna Jevne,
Director of the Hope Foundation in Edmonton, Alberta.

First published in the United Kingdom in 2004
by Jessica Kingsley Publishers
116 Pentonville Road
London N1 9JB, England
and
400 Market Street, Suite 400
Philadelphia, PA 19106, USA
www.jkp.com

Copyright © John R. Cutcliffe 2004

Library of Congress Cataloging in Publication Data

Cutcliffe, John R., 1966-
    The inspiration of hope in bereavement counselling / John R. Cutcliffe.
    p. cm.
    Includes bibliographical references and index.
    ISBN 1-84310-082-7 (alk. paper)
    1. Grief. 2. Bereavement--Psychological aspects. 3. Death--Psychological aspects. 4. Loss
(Psychology) 5. Hope. I. Title.

BF575.G7 C88 2002
155.9'37--dc21   2002021525

British Library Cataloguing in Publication Data
A CIP catalogue record for this book is available from the British Library

ISBN 1 84310 082 7

Printed and Bound in Great Britain by
Athenaeum Press, Gateshead, Tyne and Wear

Contents

Part One: Hope in Theory and Practice

Part Two: Inspiring Hope in Bereavement Counselling

Acknowledgements

This book is dedicated to the memory of my good friends, Mal Duff and Ben Clayton. Thank you for the hope you inspired in me.

I could not have completed this research without the involvement of the interviewees: the ex-clients and the therapists. Courageous people, every last one, I thank you.

My thanks go to Liz and Mike, for the supervision and support; and to Bryn and Chris for the fair and thorough examination.

Lastly, to Tracey, the epitome of a hopeful person.

Foreword

After 30 years of counselling those who have experienced loss and despairing levels of hopelessness, the complexity of the process of grieving never ceases to command my respect. There are no recipes, yet there are patterns we come to know as veterans. There are stories that tug at our hearts. There is pain we question if we could ourselves bear. Privileged to be part of a private transformation we enter a relationship intending to help.

Counselling has a complexity that will continue to unfold for decades yet to come. The human relationship including the helping relationship, remains partially in the territory of the intangible. By accepting the challenge of researching what is essentially an art, John has invited us to reflect on our practice and our science. He has risked going beyond the *what* to the *how*. In fields of disciplined inquiry there is often the temptation to make important what we can empirically study in conventional ways. The challenge accepted in the study that forms the backdrop to this book is to study what is important. Mining the tacit knowledge of experienced therapists, he has sought to make explicit what we tend to know implicitly. In so doing, he has, I believe, accurately named a core task of counselling, if not the core task.

The Inspiration of Hope in Bereavement Counselling stimulates the reflective practitioner to a multitude of questions. By questioning we enhance our capacities to be of assistance to those who suffer from loss. In this text the questions are not forced upon us but rather emerge from the interface of our counselling experience and the views presented.

John gives us the first question, 'What is hope?' After an introduction to selected views, the question arises, 'With what theoretical and philosophical stance do I align? Are there other views of hope not presented here? If I had to define hope, would I concur with the dictionary? How do my views of hope influence my practice? How does my practice influence my views of hope? What role does my training and discipline play in my view of hope? How culturally bound am I in terms of my perceptions of hope?'

Implicit in the text is the question, 'Who is the counsellor who can inspire hope?' *The Inspiration of Hope in Bereavement Counselling* speaks directly to the need for bereavement counsellors to attend to their own hope or fall prey to vicarious trauma that drains hope, like an intravenous running the wrong direction. This seldom approached topic is in the foreground of the process of inspiring hope.

The hope of the practitioner is a dimension of hope studies that is ripe for even further study. Over time each of us comes to understand that the assessment process is mutual. Not only do we assess the hope and hopelessness of our clients but they indeed are assessing whether we are hopeful enough to be useful to them. John suggests a wonderful addition to basic counselling theory. Perhaps a further core condition might be considered, that of hope and hopefulness.

In *The Inspiration of Hope in Bereavement Counselling* findings include that veteran counsellors advise not using hope as a visible construct. It is not to be named or used directly in interventions. We may agree or disagree with them. This increasingly contested discussion raises several questions: 'Where do I stand? What is my experience? If the inspiration of hope is the core of my task, how do I approach it? Am I familiar with new strategies proposed by positive psychology and hope focused counselling which use hope directly?' There is grist for many a research mill in this new field of hope studies.

John has moved us beyond simply 'hope as an outcome' to 'hope as a process' of inspiring re-engagement with life. In other words, with the progression in theory present here, hope is advanced to a theoretical framework for intervention. *Naming* the process of bereavement counselling the 'Inspiration of Hope', will perhaps take us to the cusp of yet another frontier. The question which arises is 'How might hope become a more intentional and visible part of the process?'

Professor Ronna Jevne, Director of the Hope Foundation and
Professor Emeritus, Department of Educational Psychology,
University of Alberta

References

Edey, W. and R. Jevne (2003) 'Hope Illness and Counselling Practice: Making Hope Visible.' *Canadian Journal of Counselling 37*, 1, 44–51.

Jevne, R. and J. Miller (1999) *Finding hope: Seeing the world in a brighter light.* Fort Wayne, IN: Willowgreen Press.

Nekolaichuk, C.L, Jevne, R. F. and T.O Maguire (1999) 'Structuring the meaning of hope in health and illness.' *Social Science & Medicine 48*, 591–605.

Introduction

The experience of bereavement can be considered to have a number of phases as people react to and adjust to their loss. These phases need not occur in a linear fashion, nor do they make bereavement a mechanistic process. Whilst there is much that people have in common in their experience of bereavement and loss, the experience is nevertheless unique to each individual. A person needs to reach a place of acceptance, to achieve a resolution in order to complete their bereavement. Yet all individuals do not achieve this resolution naturally. Some individuals appear to become stuck in this process; this can be described as experiencing a complicated grief reaction. Implicit in the bereavement literature is the apparent relationship with hope and hopelessness. It appears that a completed bereavement process can be linked with the re-emergence of hope and a complicated bereavement process be linked with continued hopelessness.

While many theories of bereavement counselling indicate implicitly the re-emergence of hope in the bereft individual as a result of the counselling, they do not make specific reference to how this inspiration occurs. Since the re-emergence of hope appears to be inextricably linked to a person's movement towards a completed bereavement reaction, and this movement is facilitated by means of bereavement counselling, there is a clear need to examine how this hope-inspiration occurs. This book is an attempt to move the current understanding of hope inspiration in bereavement counselling, and to answer the key question: 'Do bereavement counsellors inspire hope and if so, how?'

It is important to point out that there is currently no other book that focuses on the inspiration of hope in bereavement counselling. However, it is also necessary to stress that you do not need to be a bereavement counsellor in order to gain something from reading this text. The book has been written with the following groups of people in mind:

- counsellors, psychotherapists, psychologists
- bereavement workers (e.g. Cruse volunteers, Samaritans)
- mental health practitioners
- student/trainee counsellors, psychotherapists and psychologists
- student mental health practitioners
- voluntary counselling/helping agencies e.g. Cruse counsellors
- clerics (e.g. rabbis, ministers of other faith communities, priests and chaplains).

***

This book addresses some of the key deficits in the knowledge base, and bridges some of the important gaps that currently exist in hope-inspiration theory. The basis of the book is the emerging 'theory of the inspiration of hope in bereavement counselling' that I have developed from a qualitative study with bereavement counsellors and ex-clients, summarized in Appendix 1. Mentions in the book of such as 'the theory', 'my study' or 'my research' refer to this theory and research.

The book starts with a brief look at how hope has been regarded in philosophical and religious traditions, and in the academic healthcare literature. In Chapter 2 I set out the theory of the inspiration of hope in bereavement counselling. Chapter 3 brings the discussion round to the inspiration of hope in practice, with a particular focus on the caring professions. The full implications for practitioners are dealt with in Chapter 4, and Chapters 4, 5 and 6 describe how hope is inspired in the three phases of bereavement counselling. The implications of the theory are considered in terms of the education, research and policy issues in Chapters 7 and 8.

***

Developing the Theory

Counselling literature and mental healthcare literature contain a growing number of references to hope. The concept is gaining recognition for its influence and importance in an individual's life, and in particular domains of life; nowhere more so than the domain of health and well-being. Many key psychotherapy authors allude to the interpersonal focus of 'counselling work' (e.g. Frankl 1959; Rogers 1952) and, consequently, some counselling and nursing theory endeavours to explain and promote understanding of the person's world and the many variables that may affect it (McKenna 1997). Given the growing recognition of the importance of hope, and the purpose of counselling/nursing theory, there may be merit in examining, critiquing and attempting to understand the function, impact and influence of hope within the individual. Whilst DuFault and Martocchio (1985) have argued that most healthcare workers would agree that hope is necessary for healthy living, there is only a limited empirical literature that provides guidance for these healthcare workers about how to mobilise hope in specific client groups.

This particular substantive area was of particular interest to me because of my background as first, a psychiatric/mental health nurse, and second, as a practitioner involved with bereavement work and bereavement counselling. I wanted to address some of the deficits and to bridge some of the gaps that currently exist in hope inspiration theory (Kylma and Vehvilainen-Julkunen 1997) by carrying out research on which future care interventions could be based. It became evident that whilst work had been carried out into how to inspire hope in terminally ill individuals (Cutcliffe 1995; Herth 1990a; Miller 1989; Owen 1989), there appeared to be a dearth of research into ways of inspiring hope in bereaved individuals.

One of the most profound losses, and most significant negative life events (Holms and Rahe 1967) is the death of one's loved one. The range of experiences, emotions and responses this loss brings about in the individual are diverse and highly individualized. However, one theme repeated in the literature is that of the individual's experience of a sense of loss of their hope (Harvey *et al.* 1992; Herth 1990; Glick, Weiss and Parkes 1974; Kubler-Ross 1970; Leick and Davidsen-Nielsen 1987).

It is reasonable to suggest that most bereft individuals appear to progress through their bereavement experience without any professional healthcare input. A number of authors describe grieving as a process (DiGiulio 1992; Kubler-Ross 1970; Morgan 1994; Raphael 1982) with the eventual outcome of this process being a sense of acceptance. The individual reaches a 'place of peace', they are able to think back to their loved one without being racked with grief, 'breaking down' or experiencing this loss of hope or sense of hopelessness.

However, there are those individuals who do not progress through any process of grief. They somehow become 'stuck', unable to move past a certain point. It is likely that they have difficulty with certain tasks of grief (Crow 1991; DiGiulio 1992; Leick and Davidsen-Nielson 1987; Morgan 1994; Worden 1988) or are unwilling to let go. Carter (1989) summarized the experiences of bereaved individuals who felt stuck in time, overpowered and helpless. This led to despair in some of the individuals to the extent that several entertained thoughts of suicide. Thus, it emerges that certain individuals, for whatever reason, are unable to complete their process of grieving and so experience a 'complicated' grief reaction, and that these individuals may well undergo a prolonged loss of hope or sense of hopelessness.

The discipline of counselling is moving towards becoming an evidence-based practice discipline in that interventions, policies and procedures are beginning to be based on research and evidence (Barkham 1996; McKenna 1997). It is necessary to have theory to support one's interventions, and this theory may need to be induced: that is, where there is a lack of theory to date, qualitative enquiry is required to generate new knowledge and new theories need to occur.

PART ONE

Hope in Theory and Practice

1

What is Hope?

The *Collins English Dictionary* defines 'hope' (n.) as *expectation* and *desire*, and 'hope' (vb.) as *to hope, to expect*. The word 'hopeless' means to be without hope. Two words from the Latin for 'hopeless' are despair and desperation. Throughout this book the words 'hopelessness' and 'despair' will be interchangeable; both defining the individual as in a state of being without hope.

Philosophical background and origins

Where does hope come from? What is its origin? It is worth conducting a brief examination of some of the theological and philosophical literature for explanations.

Chinese perspective

According to Landrum (1993), whilst the early Chinese believed that human destiny depended on the gods, they also recognized the value of human virtue. Their four basic human qualities: love, righteousness, propriety and wisdom, are developed through moral training and social education. Chinese culture has a strong sense of optimism because human nature is considered to be essentially good. No specific reference to the origin of hope is made, or reference to the role hope plays. However, one could speculate that optimism is an expression of hope, albeit couched in different terminology.

East Indian perspective

Landrum (1993) asserts that an East Indian perspective is concerned with the notions of the subjective nature of humans, the value of knowing oneself, the links between the supreme inward reality of spirit and the outward reality of matter. This perspective sees the universe as being in a meaningful and constant state of flux, that yet, paradoxically, provides order. To survive, one must act. No specific reference to the origin of hope is made, or reference to the role hope has.

Ancient Greek perspective

When describing the ancient Greek perspective, Landrum (1993) suggests the early ancient Greeks regarded people as individuals who received feelings and ideas from external sources. The soul allowed understanding and, consequently, direction in life. The mind and body were viewed as separate and several human qualities and physiological responses were explained in relation to man's psyche, with reason regarded as the dominant part of psyche. Reference is made to courage, truth, and temperance, and Hippocrates alludes to the positive effects of these qualities and hope, without ever dwelling on or exploring the actual processes of hoping (Barnard 1995).

Christian perspective

If hope is considered in terms of the Christian faith then it can be argued that hope has existed almost as long as humankind has existed. This existence began when God created Adam and Eve. Adam knew nothing but contentment, satisfaction and exhilaration and consequently his existence can be seen as a hopeful one. He was in a state of contemplation; he lived the beginning of his life in the presence of God and, therefore, experienced the total absence of despair. Once Adam, through eating forbidden fruit, was alienated from God, the reality of his own demise or annihilation, or permanent separation from God, had to be faced. How did he reconcile his eventual demise and separation from his creator? How if not but by the action of faith in God (and subsequent redemption) producing a sense of hope that the state of contemplation could be achieved again?

For those who hold Christian beliefs, hope then would seem to be a product of faith (Lynch 1965), whereby individuals engage in a process in which their beliefs in their ultimate salvation, and also their empowerment in the present, are dependent on God. This faith enables these individuals to be hopeful and this hopefulness enables individuals to transcend their current difficulties (Lynch 1965) – not only in terms of their eventual redemption, but also in a pragmatic sense, in that, despite his fall from grace, not only does Adam eventually achieve his reconciliation with his creator, but in addition enjoys a long and fruitful existence.

Existential perspective

This book is concerned with hope in a specific situation; a situation in which the individual experiences and exists in an 'extreme' life experience. Within the finite existential scenario of bereavement, what does hope do? Existentialism can be regarded as the philosophy of despair; the opposite to hope. For example, Jean-Paul Sartre (1943) argued that to be truly human is to travel a path towards nihilism – alone. The more acutely aware a person is of this existence, the more aware he becomes of its absurdity. The only outcome of such a perspective is a state of despair. However, some existential literature attempts to explain how hope is derived and shares commonalities with the theological perspectives outlined above. The existentialist philosopher Marcel (1948) has proposed that humans achieve being by engaging as fully as possible in life tasks. Such tasks require communication and interaction between people. This existence has endless possibilities and opportunities for personal growth, and of increasing human stature by existing in conjunction with other human beings. Accordingly, humankind has wide horizons that they can move towards and influence, as opposed to Sartre's view of humanity as being surrounded by a sea of nothingness. Therefore, if despair is the state of being of Sartre's man, hopefulness (and the potential to be hopeful) is the state of being of Marcel's man.

Hope in the healthcare literature

From the 1960s onwards there have been numerous attempts to define and understand hope in the theoretical and empirical literature.

Lynch (1965) described the spiritual view of hope. Writing in the position of a reverend and as someone who had ministered to many people in times of distress, he suggested hope comes close to being the very centre of humanity. Stotland (1969), writing from a psychological perspective, indicated that even though there was an awareness of the role hopefulness plays in everyday life, the subject had not been fully introduced into the mainstream of psychology and psychiatry.

In the 1980s studies were conducted to define hope in specific groups. Hinds (1984) attempted this with adolescents. She constructed a definition of hope, stating that hope is the degree to which an adolescent believes that a personal tomorrow exists, and arguing that this belief spans four hierarchical levels, from lower to higher levels of believing:

1. Forced effort: the degree to which an adolescent tries artificially to take on a more positive view.

2. Personal possibilities: the extent to which an adolescent believes that second chances for the self may exist.

3. Expectation of a better tomorrow: the degree to which an adolescent has a positive, though non-specific, future orientation.

4. Anticipation of a personal future: the extent to which an adolescent identifies specific and personal future possibilities.

DuFault and Martocchio (1985) collected data over two years from elderly cancer patients, then collected similar data over a further two years from terminally ill patients of various ages. They claimed to have identified two spheres of hope:

1. Generalized hope: hopes that are broad in scope, not linked to any particular object of hope, e.g. I don't hope for anything in particular, I just hope.

2. Particularized hope: hopes that are concerned with a valued outcome, state of being, that is a hope object, e.g. improvement in health, passing an exam.

They also described six dimensions of hope, each of which is depicted by a set of components that structure the experience of hope. Each of the dimensions of hope can belong to both generalized and particularised hope. They describe these dimensions as:

1. affective – focusing on sensations and emotions that are part of the hoping process

2. cognitive – focusing on the processes by which individuals wish, imagine, wonder, perceive, think, remember, learn, generalize, interpret and judge in relation to hope

3. behavioural – focusing on the action orientation of the hoping person in relation to hope

4. affiliative – focusing on the person's hoping sense of relatedness or involvement beyond self as it bears upon hope

5. temporal – focusing on the hoping person's experience of time (past, present and future) in relation to hope and hoping

6. contextual – focusing on how hope is brought to the forefront of awareness and experience within the context of life as interpreted by the hoping person.

DuFault and Martocchio (1985) draw these elements together to define hope as:

> A multidimensional dynamic life force characterized by a confident yet uncertain expectation of achieving a future good which, to the hoping person, is realistically possible and personally significant. (p.380)

From a study of clinical nurse specialists caring for cancer patients, Owen (1989) developed a conceptual model of hope in such patients. The model comprised six themes:

1. Goal setting – hopeful patients engaged in setting (and revising) attainable goals. It may be worth noting that the goals of these patients noticeably changed as death approached (e.g. smaller, more attainable, more realistic).

2. Positive personal attributes – hopeful patients were described as having several hopeful personality characteristics (e.g. courage, optimism and a positive attitude).

3.	Future redefinition – hopeful patients were described as those who saw or perceived the future, and this future was not quantified in time.

4.	Meaning in life – hopeful patients were those who equated hope with a meaningful life.

5.	Peace – hopeful patients were described as being at peace or comfortable with their situation.

6.	Energy – hopeful patients were described as being those who possessed and gave out energy. Additionally, Owen reported that the hopeful patient needed energy to remain hopeful, hope required energy and gave energy.

Prior to these inductive studies, Miller (1983) had drawn together the relevant literature on hope in order to define what hope is, and how it can be inspired in those people with chronic illness. The following alleged key elements of hope were identified:

1.	valued

2.	private (personalized)

3.	powerful

4.	an intrinsic component of life

5.	providing dynamism for the spirit

6.	an expectation

7.	an inner readiness

8.	central to human existence ('Everything human beings do in life is central to life' (p.287)).

During the 1990s further attempts were made to define hope and build upon the existing theory and knowledge. Stephenson (1991) reviewed 52 theoretical and empirical papers that focused on hope. This review included the empirical work that had been carried out during the 1980s, perhaps offering a more comprehensive understanding than Miller's (1983) work (as a result of including the more recent empirical work).

Stephenson's (1991) concept analysis identified nine conceptual attributes of hope and these described hope as:

1. a basic human response

2. providing a meaning in life

3. a process

4. having a developmental component (it is dynamic, not static)

5. being future-orientated

6. an element of anticipation

7. a multidimensional concept

8. being associated with nursing

9. being a theory.

Stephenson (1991) concludes her concept analysis by defining hope as:

> A process of anticipation that involves the interaction of thinking, acting, feeling and relating, and is directed towards a future fulfilment that is personally meaningful. (p.1459)

In 1995 Morse and Doberneck claimed that, despite previous research efforts, the concept of hope remained poorly understood, and suggested that previous attempts at concept development have not produced significant results. They claimed that Stephenson's (1991) attributes are so abstract that they lose their unique association with hope and may be applied to other concepts, such as friendship. Consequently, Morse and Doberneck (1995) undertook a concept analysis of hope, using the methods of concept analysis described in Morse and Doberneck (1995). Their description of the concept of hope was developed using interview data from four participating groups: patients undergoing heart transplant, patients with spinal cord injuries, breast cancer survivors, and breast-feeding mothers. Their analysis identified seven abstract and universal components of hope:

1. a realistic initial assessment of the predicament or threat

2. the envisioning of alternatives and the setting of goals

3. a bracing for negative outcomes

4.   a realistic assessment of personal resources and of external conditions and resources

5.   the socialisation of mutually supportive relationships

6.   the continuous evaluation for signs that reinforce the selected goals

7.   a determination to endure.

Although the concept of hope has been discussed in healthcare literature since the 1960s, it is still difficult to find one definition that encapsulates all that hope is and specifically how it relates to health, disease and healthcare. What is evident is that many of these studies seem to have captured or identified some elements of the phenomenon we call hope. The key elements of these definitions of hope are summarized in Table 1.1.

As stated previously, there is evidence in the literature that indicates that the current understanding of the areas of hope and hoping for particular client groups is incomplete. Consequently, the areas of hope and hoping for these client groups can be regarded as ones where theory needs to be induced. From the initial brief examination of the literature, it is implicit that hope, loss of hope and hopelessness appear to be bound up with an unresolved or complicated bereavement reaction. Therefore, the individuals in this client group appear to have an implicit need for hope inspiration.

The possibility of this implicit relationship led me to the key question: do bereavement counsellors inspire hope in their clients and if so, how? Therefore, it became apparent that there was a need to carry out research that investigates if there is an element of hope inspiration within bereavement counselling; and if so, to identify the dynamics, principles and basic social and psychosocial processes involved (Schultz 1967) and thus have evidence on which to base future interventions. This research, summarized in Appendix I, gave rise to the theory of the inspiration of hope in bereavement counselling.

Table 1.1 Summary of the key elements of definitions of hope in the healthcare literature

	Multi-dimensional	Dynamic	Central to life	Future orientated	individualized	Process	Goal Setting	Associated with nursing
DuFault and Martocchio (1985)	Yes	Yes	Yes (life force)	Yes (future good)	Yes (personally significant)	No	No	Yes (social dimension)
Hinds (1984)	No	Yes	Yes	Yes (personal tomorrow)	Yes (personal tomorrow)	No	Yes	No
Owen (1989)	Yes	Yes (focus of hope changes)	Yes (meaning, peace, energy)	Yes (future redefinition)	Yes (positive personal attributes)	No	Yes	No
Miller (1983)	Yes	Yes	Yes	Yes	Yes (private)	No	No	No
Stephenson (1991)	Yes	Yes	Yes	Yes	Yes	Yes	Yes	Yes
Morse and Doberneck (1995)	Yes	Yes	No	Yes	Yes	Yes	Yes	No

The theory

The integrated theory of the inspiration of hope in bereavement counselling is comprised of one core variable (hope inspiration) and three sub-core variables; these sub-core variables describe the 'stages' or 'phases' to this process of hope inspiration. The sub-core variables comprise these three phases:

1. forging the connection and the relationship

2. facilitating a cathartic release

3. experiencing a healthy [good] ending.

There is a sense of temporality; a linear movement from the first phase, through the second and subsequently completing with the third phase. While it is clear that there is progression through these phases, there are also smaller 'cyclic' processes within. These are perhaps best described as being analogous to the wave motion associated with the movement of the tide. There is a gradual and progressive movement through the phases of hope inspiration; however at times the 'forward' movement is counter balanced with movement 'backwards'.

PHASE ONE	PHASE TWO	PHASE THREE
FORGING THE CONNECTION AND RELATIONSHIP	FACILITATING A CATHARTIC RELEASE	EXPERIENCING A HEALTHY [GOOD] ENDING

THE IMPLICIT PROJECTION OF HOPE AND HOPEFULNESS

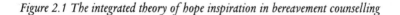

Figure 2.1 The integrated theory of hope inspiration in bereavement counselling

The key psychosocial process of hope inspiration in bereavement counselling is ever present. This omnipresent psychosocial process thus allows us to think of this as the key to answering the research question. In answering the question, how the bereavement counsellor inspires hope wll be partly dependent on where he/she is within this process.

Simultaneously, irrespective of where the counsellors are within the process, they will be able to inspire hope using the core variable: the implicit projection of hope and hopefulness.

The theory indicates that forging the connection, engaging the client and forming the relationship, are the initial stage of the process. Hope is inspired during this initial stage as a result of five processes, namely:

1. experiencing a caring, human–human connection

2. countering the projection of hopelessness

3. unwavering commitment

4. rediscovering trust

5. permeating hope throughout the counselling encounter.

Once the client and counsellor have established a connection and relationship, once the clients have a sense of trust in their counsellor, then they are able to move onto the next stage or phase of the process – that is, the phase of facilitating a cathartic release. The transition into this second stage does not indicate that the process of engagement and relationship formation is complete or that it finishes. What it does indicate, however, is that the basic processes appear to shift in emphasis from forming the engagement/connection to facilitating a cathartic release. Hope is inspired during this second stage as a result of seven processes, namely:

1. facilitating the release of painful emotion

2. supplying the opportunity for reflection

3. providing unconditional and continual support

4. freeing the client to talk about the deceased

5. employing therapeutic touch

6. purposefully utilising silence

7. avoiding colluding with the client's denial and/or hopelessness.

As the client ventilates their emotional pain within a safe, caring, and hopeful atmosphere, they begin to move towards ending. It is again important to note that movement into the third stage does not imply that the client has no more emotional pain to express. However, what it does indicate is that the basic processes appear to shift in emphasis from expressing painful emotions to working towards, and experiencing, a healthy ending. Particular attention is given in the therapy to the timing and manner of ending as a means of hope inspiration, and this inspiration occurs as a result of five processes, namely:

1. realising the potential for growth in bereavement

2. avoiding repeats

3. accomplishing any tasks of bereavement

4. ensuring clients retain control

5. increasing the client's self-awareness.

Whilst clients move through these three stages or phases of hope inspiration in bereavement counselling, there is simultaneously another basic psychosocial process occurring, and this process is evident throughout the duration of the therapy: it is the implicit projection of hope and hopefulness.

Counsellors are responsible for bringing hope into the therapy, and this is projected into both the counselling 'atmosphere' and the client. However, all of this projection is purposefully implicit rather than overt. Clients are able to 'pick up' and 'take on board' the emotions projected into the counselling atmosphere. Furthermore, as a result of the multidimensional connection formed between the client and counsellor, a transplantation of hope occurs. Hope appears to be transplanted from the counsellor, via the spiritual connection, to the client.

The counsellor's hope and hopefulness is not limited to any particular phase of the therapy. It is there at the start, it remains there during the therapy, and it is still there as the therapy draws towards an ending. Despite hope being ever present, it is not referred to explicitly. However, there is a continual implicit sense of hope for the counsellor and this is introduced, implicitly, into each encounter, and as a result, at the end of the therapy the clients possess some of this hope for themselves, as will be seen in Part Two of this book.

PART TWO

Inspiring Hope in Bereavement Counselling

2

How Hope Works

Theory into Practice

The analysis of my research data indicates that the inspiration of hope in bereavement counselling appears to occur as a result of the sense of being cared about, the human–human interpersonal connection, and the external help provided by the counsellor. Consequently, we need to examine

- links between hope inspiration and caring
- the interpersonal nature of hope inspiration.

Caring, carers and hope inspiration

The existing literature shows that whilst it can be considered as the final interior resource of man, hope alone cannot sustain its own existence forever (e.g. Lynch 1965). This can be seen to be the case especially if its energy is being used to feed and support the individual. It is not a limitless resource: eventually these resources of hope will be exhausted, for otherwise nobody would ever become hopeless. Participants in my research allude to this limited supply of personal hope and, in particular, to the way in which clients in need of bereavement counselling for complicated grief appeared to have depleted most of their own hope 'reserves'.

Lynch (1965) maintains that hope is nurtured by help from outside agencies:

> Hope is a relative idea, it is relative to the idea of help, it seeks help, it depends, it looks to the outside world. (p.12)

Lynch does not specify the source of help, only that it is external to the individual. His theory appears to posit that an individual is unable to make themselves experience a greater sense of hopefulness, since their personal hope levels depend on external interaction. However, other studies conclude that individuals can make some attempts to maintain their own hope level. For example, terminally ill cancer patients used their personal attributes and uplifting memories to maintain their hope (Herth 1990), patients undergoing repeated renal dialysis identified devising and revising goals as helping to maintain their hope (Miller 1983), and patients who had been hospitalized in a critical care unit coped by means of having the attitude of determinism (Miller 1989). It is also reasonable to suggest that some people will have a greater innate level of hope than others. Since all human beings are unique, they have different personal resources, qualities and characteristics in varying intensities, one individual's personal resource of hope being perhaps greater than another's.

Whilst there do appear to be some strategies for hope inspiration that do not require external help, these strategies are usually used in conjunction with others that do depend on external help. Furthermore, the strategies with the most influence/impact involve external help of some nature: for example, family support, nursing intervention and religious beliefs (Miller and Wake 1992; Raleigh 1992). Thus, despite the possibility that there may be some people who are naturally more hopeful than others, even their hope looks to the outside, for external help. People who have survived in extreme conditions after an accident, imprisonment or after becoming stranded, for example, Holocaust survivors (Frankl 1959), often speak of hanging on until help came or, conversely, looking to their faith and particular belief in God.

Other authors support the link between hope and help. Cutcliffe and Grant (2001) stress that it is impossible to discuss hope without mentioning help. Hope is inside us; it is the interior feeling that there is help on the outside.

As already mentioned, it appears that whilst individuals can to a certain extent maintain their own hope level, this cannot go on indefinitely. Eventually the resource of hope will be depleted as it sustains the individual and the intrapersonal strategies of hope inspiration become less effective. This in turn creates the need for external help in order to replenish the individual's hope and support the intrapersonal, hope-inspiring strategies.

To consider this link in terms of the theological/philosophical standpoint described in Chapter 1, hope's first seeking for help was directed towards God. People needed help in order to achieve the position of contemplation and subsequently to become hopeful. Whilst this help is of a spiritual nature, it remains help external to the individual.

The spiritual source of external help is not the sole source. Helping patients takes many forms, and one can regard all forms of counselling and nursing intervention as external help. If external help does indeed promote higher hope levels, it can be argued that external help in the specific form of counselling or nursing interventions should also produce higher hope levels. It is evident that an intrinsic component of nursing is helping the patient, whatever form this help takes. It is also evident that external help is inextricably linked to hope, with external help being a source of hope inspiration. It is logical to suggest that nursing, in the form of external help, is therefore inseparable from hope inspiration, just as my emerging theory of hope inspiration suggests that external help in the form of bereavement counselling is hope-inspiring.

Furthermore, if hope is relative to help, if hope seeks help, then the hopeful person can reasonably be expected to seek out help in order to remain hopeful. Perhaps this seeking for hope would be most noticeable when the normally hopeful person feels that their hope is compromised. One could postulate that such searching may not occur when the individual's hope level is extremely compromised. Perhaps help needs to be forthcoming within a certain undefined time limit. If action directed to finding external help is prompted initially by internal hope, it perhaps follows that the individual needs to have some internal hope in order to seek help. This interactive relationship between hope and help can be seen in those people who experience profound hopelessness as they appear to do nothing to help themselves (Aldridge 1998; Bruss 1988; Rawlins 1993). They are listless and apathetic. They do not often seek out external help; in effect the help needs to come to them.

Peplau (1988) conceptualized nursing as a therapeutic, interpersonal process in which the service offered by nurses is to help individuals understand their health problems. More recently Barker (1997) concluded that psychiatric and mental health nursing involves the provision of necessary conditions under which people may review their experiences, and is focused on helping people live. Helping, assisting, aiding, whatever word is chosen to describe this, all include the idea of the therapist or nurse interacting with the patient and making a difference. The individual is somehow different after their interaction with the therapist or nurse as a result of external help. This difference might not be a tangible or visible phenomenon, but change will have occurred. What becomes evident from examining the literature is that another change occurs when a therapist/nurse helps a patient, and that is a change in their hope level. In the same way that recipients of nursing care have identified nurses as giving them hope, the ex-clients in this study have identified the counsellors and the bereavement counselling as a source of hope.

Help can be viewed as the action component of a caring relationship. What begins to become evident is that caring and helping are inextricably linked and together they form central constructs of the nature of nursing.

In an earlier study (Cutcliffe 1995) I attempted to elicit how nurses inspire and instil hope in terminally ill HIV clients. I described four categories of hope inspiration:

1.   Affirmation of worth: the nurse communicates to the client that she deems them to have worth and value. The demonstration of unconditional acceptance and tolerance.

2.   Reflection in action: the presence and application of self-awareness and reflection in the nurse.

3.   Creation of a partnership: the nurse and the client enter into a partnership where decision-making is a democratic process, care is negotiated rather than just something done to someone.

4.   The totality of the person: the consideration of the client in a holistic sense.

These findings suggest that hope inspiration is a subtle, unobtrusive process, interwoven with the same subtle act of caring. This process involves the presence of another human being who demonstrates unconditional acceptance, tolerance and understanding, and consequently enters into caring practice and simultaneously inspires hope.

Arguments have been constructed that suggest the way individuals are treated has an influence ultimately on how these individuals feel about themselves (Peplau 1988; Rogers 1952, 1957). There are a multitude of messages communicated by the attitude, demeanour and approach adopted by the nurse. Non-verbal communication is a powerful way of communicating. Argyle (1975) argues that up to 80 per cent of communication is non-verbal and Duck (1992) develops this argument, asserting that people respond to non-verbal more than they do to verbal communication. This is especially the case if there is any incongruence between the verbal and non-verbal communication.

Thus, if a client senses that a nurse is uninterested and uncaring, the effect on their feelings of self-worth is likely to be a negative one (Benner and Wrubel 1989). A subliminal message of hopelessness is also communicated (Cutcliffe 1996). In effect the nurse indicates subliminally: 'What is the point in engaging or reaching out to you? Why should I bother? There is no hope ' Such non-verbal communications are likely to convey a message of hopelessness that may have an effect on the patient's hope level (Cutcliffe 1995; Herth 1990). The nurse then needs to examine his/her own attitude, lest hopelessness and the absence of a caring attitude are communicated empathically. My earlier research (Cutcliffe 1996) further supports the link between hope and caring – how the actions and non-verbal communication of the nurse influences patients' levels of hope.

Benner's (1984) eight competencies of the nursing helping role includes creating a climate for, and establishing a commitment to, healing. According to Benner, a crucial component of this process is the mobilisation of hope for the client and the nurse. She goes on to provide a clinical example of how such hope is mobilised. In this example a nurse is involved in the care of a client with breast cancer. The nurse describes how she conceptualized a particular, optimistic future for the client based on her successful experience of caring for similar clients. This hope is then projected by means of understanding the client's perspective, encouraging the client to be more assertive, to form shared goals, and is offered in all that the nurse does with and for the client.

Miller (1989) attempted to explore strategies that critically ill persons used to maintain or increase their hope status while confronting a life-threatening event. Nine hope-inspiring categories emerged from the study:

1. Cognitive strategies – using thought processes to buffer threatening perceptions.

2. Mental attitude of determinism – having a conviction in a positive outcome.

3. Philosophy of life – feeling that life has meaning and growth results from crises; experiencing genuine optimism.

4. Spiritual strategies – having beliefs and practices enabling transcendence of suffering.

5. Relationships with caregivers – receiving from caregivers a constructive view of patient, expectations of patient's ability to manage difficulty, and confidence in therapy.

6. Family bond – having sustaining relationships with loved ones.

7. Sense of being in control – having a sense that one's knowledge and actions can affect an outcome.

8. Goal accomplishment – having desired activities and outcomes to attain.

9. Miscellaneous strategies – having other specific coping behaviours that thwart feelings of despair, including distraction and humour.

Miller's 5th and 6th strategies clearly refer to the value of *support*, from family/significant others and by caregivers, as a means of hope inspiration.

In an attempt to explore the meaning of hope, Herth (1990) identified strategies that are used to foster hope in terminally ill adults. This comprehensive study produced seven categories of hope-fostering strategies and three hope-hindering categories:

Hope-fostering categories

1. Interpersonal connectedness – presence of a meaningful relationship(s) with another person(s).

2. Lightheartedness – feeling of delight, joy or playfulness that is communicated verbally or non-verbally.

3. Personal attributes – those of determinism, courage and serenity.

4. Attainable aims – directing efforts at some purpose.

5. Spiritual base – presence of active spiritual beliefs and practices.

6. Uplifting memories – recalling positive moments/times.

7. Affirmation of worth – having one's individuality accepted, honoured and acknowledged.

Hope-hindering categories

1. Abandonment and isolation – physical and/or emotional loss of significant others.

2. Uncontrollable pain or discomfort – continuance of overwhelming pain or discomfort despite repeated attempts to control.

3. Devaluation of personhood – being treated as a non-person of little value.

Again, there are correspondences here with my own findings, in particular the 6th hope-fostering category (*uplifting memories*) and the 2nd hope-hindering category (*freeing clients from pain*). Herth (1990) also suggests that *the use of touch* perhaps restores a sense of human-centred dignity and hopefulness.

Temporal dimensions of hope

My research with counsellors and ex-clients indicates that the inspiration of hope in bereavement counselling appears to have distinct phases or stages to the process. There is evidence of a temporal dimension to the inspiration of hope theory, in that three of the stages occurred in sequence. Whilst these stages were not absolute (i.e. the boundaries overlapped one another), there was a distinct sense of the client moving from a position of relative hopelessness to one of relative hopefulness. Similarly, clients began to perceive the future more, and thought of their future in more hopeful ways. Also, the participants described the changes in the hope level of the clients, and the nature or focus of the clients' hope, through the process of bereavement counselling.

Hope appears to be concerned with the future. When an individual has hope they consider the future in one form or another. Previous scenarios in the individual's past, in which hope was implicitly or explicitly enabling, can certainly be drawn upon. This can be seen particularly with regard to the sphere of particularised hope (e.g. hope to pass a test, achieve a certain goal). However, even in this situation it is the application of past coping that enables the 'here and now' and the future to be conceptualized in a positive manner. For example, the hopeful person may use past successes (e.g. exam success) to help sustain hope in the present about forthcoming exams. Thus, hope has a future orientation, and the individual hopes that the future will be better than the present. Alternatively, it is concerned with hoping that the current difficulties end, that present issues are coped with more easily in the future and that the future is therefore more appealing. It becomes evident, therefore, that the individual who has hope is not looking solely at their current circumstances and problems, but is conceptualizing ways out, or simply believing that there is a way out.

Lynch (1965) propounds that wishing and hoping are inextricably linked. When we cannot wish, we cannot hope. This illustrates further the future orientation of hope. To wish is to long for, desire and to want something to happen. Even when people speak of wishing they had (or had not) done something in the past, this is so that their 'here and now' and their personal future will be more appealing. Whilst the event they wish to alter occurred in the past, the consequences of the event occur in the present and the future.

If this is the case, if hopeful people focus more on the future and give only cursory attention to the past, then it should follow that hopeless people will focus on the past and give only cursory attention to the future. Lynch (1965) described people in a condition of hopelessness as being 'bogged down' in the past, unable to see any future, with their situation becoming fixed, absolute. Hopelessness is then a sense of the impossible, it is a sense of pointlessness, futility. Statements akin to 'Why bother? Nothing will change' abound in the hopeless person. Further evidence for this is provided by Frankl's (1959) accounts of life in a Nazi concentration camp during the Second World War. There he observed that when a person lost hope he or she could no longer cope and consequently did not live long.

In an attempt to differentiate hopelessness from helplessness and powerlessness, Drew (1990) provides a clinical example of a person exhibiting hopelessness. The individual in this example is described as being hesitant and withdrawn; she has lost the meaning in her life, she perceives herself as weak, as a failure. Miller (1983) supports this viewpoint, suggesting that people in a state of hopelessness will make little or no effort towards setting future goals and plans emphasising current failures and verbalising doubts about themselves, their care and their lives. The emphasis and focus is on the past.

However, Bruss (1988) contends that hopeless individuals do consider the future, but their future is perceived as dismal and bleak. The argument highlighting the future orientation of hope does not submit that individuals experiencing hopelessness never contemplate or mention the future. It is more that most of their thoughts will be directed to the past, where their temporal focus is. Although hopeful people are future orientated, they will of course mention the past.

Whilst the orientation is towards the future, there is important evidence that suggests the product of this hope is evident in the individual's 'here and now'. In my study of coronary care clients (Cutcliffe 1996), participants verbalized that hope was a resource for them that helped them cope with their current suffering. The interviewees described this in the following ways:

Having hope enables me to think that I will improve, get better.

Having hope means that this is not the end, it is only temporary.

(p.869)

Thus, from examination of the literature it begins to emerge that the difficulties or stressors the individual experiences in the present can be overcome by having hope for the future. Hope for the future is then manifested in the holistic well-being of the person in the present.

Hope appears to be a dynamic rather than a static phenomenon. Personal hope levels fluctuate over time (e.g. Herth 1990). Vaillot (1970) describes how, following a severe cerebrovascular accident, the family of an 82-year-old woman were informed by the medics that their mother would never recover. She would remain bedridden, her pneumonia would only get worse, in short this was the end. Despite this prognosis the nurses evidently remained hopeful about the care of this client. In fact, she appeared to regain a degree of hope, became a more hopeful person, began to focus on the future rather than the past, and was eventually discharged home. Hope was not static throughout her hospitalisation but responded and grew as a result of nursing care.

In adult life our particularised hopes often change in accordance with what we deem to be of value at that particular juncture in life. For example, the individual with forthcoming examinations or a driving test is likely to have these events as the focus of their particularised hopes. Once a successful outcome has been achieved the individual is likely to begin hoping for something else, e.g. a new job, a new car.

Moreover, perhaps the most poignant indication of the changing nature of an individual's hope is evident in terminally ill individuals. Essentially, the individual's focus of hope becomes more attuned to the spiritual dimension and, additionally, hope for their significant others (Farran, Salloway and Clark 1990; Herth 1990). The previously mentioned study of hope inspiration in terminally ill people by Herth (1990) described how these individuals shifted the focus of their hope. Hoping became associated less with achievement within a specific time, less specific and more global, and especially less focused on self and more on significant others. Additionally, hopes for the dying individual often became more 'spiritually' and less physically focused.

> Some older persons readily indicate then when they think of the future they think more of 'a life in the hereafter', as opposed to a future life on earth. (Farran, Salloway and Clark 1990, p.52)

The actual process of hoping is also dynamic. The way in which an individual hopes changes throughout his life. Just as the individual develops, so does the process of hoping. As alluded to earlier, Erickson (1964) describes how hope first arises during the first stage of infant development, specifically as trust versus mistrust. Hope for the infant is centred around having his basic needs met. Arguably, the infant hasn't developed sufficiently in cognitive terms to involve his imagination at this stage. However, as one becomes more cognitively developed, the process of hoping involves more cognition and becomes more complex, with specific strategies utilized. Hoping, therefore, begins as a subconscious process and develops into a conscious one.

The centrality of hope

Whilst I identified the projection of hope and hopefulness as central to the emerging theory, it remained implicit. Hope can be viewed as a basic, fundamental and integral part of everyday life and this warrants further exploration. Many authors describe the centrality of hope (e.g. Lynch 1965; Marcel 1948). St Paul wrote of hope being integral to life, a basic human response. Indeed, Vaillot (1970) argues that hope springs from the depths of one's being.

It appears, then, that there is a well-established argument that posits hope as being central to life, central to existence and interwoven with one's spiritual centre, one's soul. If this is indeed the case, then the absence of hope (i.e. hopelessness) will be manifest in the individual in the form of complete despair (hopelessness and despair being one and the same). Aldridge (1998) constructs similar arguments when he outlines the link between suicide and hopelessness. In this book Aldridge first illustrates how many factors, e.g. extent of personal relationships, socio-economic variables, family ties, medical treatment, each contribute to a person's decision to commit suicide. Then he describes how hope is inextricably bound up with each of these factors, e.g. the absence of close interpersonal relationships is likely to have a negative influence on a person's hope. Consequently, he concludes that the hopelessness located within the individual can lead to suicide and that this loss of hope results from a background of isolation, neglect, conflict and social disruption.

If hope is central to life, it follows that, where there is a sense of prolonged and never-ending despair in the individual, death will ultimately follow. Drawing together several strands of literature that attempted to explain hope, Miller (1983) argues that there appears to be a cyclical relationship involving powerlessness, depression, low self-esteem, immobilisation, hopelessness and death. She asserts that this cycle can continue until the continued hopelessness leads to death. Stapleton (1983) supports this argument, suggesting that chronic illness can give rise to a sense of powerlessness in the individual. If this powerlessness is not dealt with and continues unchecked, eventually the individual will die.

Hope does more than merely enable man to continue his existence. This is particularly the case when the individual is faced with a stressor, be it a problem to resolve, illness, or death of a family member. In order to determine what mechanisms they used to maintain or decrease their hope while confronting a life-threatening event, Miller (1989) studied people who had been critically ill. The patients in her study identified hope-inspiring and hope-hindering categories, and described themselves as being in a winning position whilst they still had hope.

Also in my previously mentioned study (Cutcliffe 1996), coronary care patients felt that their hope enabled them to cope with their current circumstances and to believe that they would transcend their current difficulties. Thus, there is evidence to indicate that, in addition to enabling the person to exist, hope provides the platform on which more positive adjustment to his/her current difficulties can be experienced.

The centrality of hope to existence can also be seen when one considers the human lifespan. Arguments can be constructed which attest that hope can be seen as a life force or sense of being that stays with us throughout our lifespan. The infant soon learns to live in hope that crying will produce a response from its carers that will meet its immediate needs. As alluded to earlier, healthy adolescents develop this sense of hope (and process of hoping) and define hope as a belief that a personal tomorrow exists (Hinds 1984). Adults of various ages and health status hope (Miller 1989; Herth 1992), and dying or terminally ill individuals still have hope (Herth 1990; Cutcliffe 1995). Terminally ill cancer patients perhaps provided a clearer understanding of the hoping process during the dying trajectory (Herth 1990). Herth's study illustrates how the focus of the hopes of the terminally ill individuals shifted as their death approached, moving from hopes for their own continued physical existence and longevity to hopes which were concerned with the well-being of their significant others, their own continued spiritual existence and life after death. The centrality of hope is therefore emphasised since it can be seen as central to life throughout the entirety of one's lifespan and perhaps even beyond.

However, despite its centrality hope can be easily overlooked, and maybe this centrality is implicit. Arguably, the presence of hope at the centre of one's being is so fundamental to existence and, more important, to an increased quality of existence, that its presence, influence and centrality can be overlooked or taken for granted. One does not draw breath and consciously hope that this sustains one's physical well-being: this is taken for granted. Yet one breathes in the unconscious hope that the air inspired will sustain life (Lynch 1965). Hope need not be viewed solely as a resource that sustains us in a crisis, but as a sense of being, a life force that is present in every moment of our existence (Vaillot 1970). Conceivably it is when the individual's health status is compromised that this internal resource becomes more apparent. It is when the individual realizes they are in need of hope that hope becomes more clear to them. Hoping then becomes more a conscious than a subconscious process.

Signs of increased hope in the client

At this stage in the development of the theory of hope inspiration in bereavement counselling, a criticism that could be levelled is: how does one know that the client has more hope as a result of engaging in bereavement counselling? Similarly, a counsellor or therapist who is considering using the theory in his or her practice may have similar questions: does this theory make any difference? In response to such questions, there are perhaps two forms of evidence that would substantiate the theory – quantitative evidence and qualitative evidence.

At this stage of the development of the theory, there is not yet any quantitative evidence that indicates a direct causal relationship between the posited theory of hope inspiration in bereavement counselling and increased levels or measures of hope in the clients. However, such a position is entirely in keeping with models of theory development (Dickoff and James 1968; Popper 1965), wherein a theory is first induced using a qualitative method, and subsequently tested using a deductive, quantitative method. It is important to note, however, that the absence of quantitative evidence does not mean there is a complete absence of evidence. My own research summarized in Appendix I alone provides both qualitative and case-study evidence. For now, if we refer to the key elements of hope identified in Chapter 1, and then examine the evidence

Table 2.1 Key elements of hope compared with interviewee statements

Key Element of Hope	Interviewee evidence / statement
Multi-dimensional	'At the end of the therapy I felt like I was in a different place, a higher point, a different sense of myself.'
Dynamic	'At the end of the therapy, I ended up at a higher point, a more hopeful point, than I had ever been before.'
Empowering	'She started to achieve specific tasks associated with her loss, i.e., attending her father's grave on Father's Day.'
Central to life	'Towards the end of the therapy the client would use words like "joy" and "celebration".'
Related to external help	'The clients were motivated to come back to therapy every week, and spoke of the therapy as an (external) source of help/hope.'
Related to caring	'I would leave the therapy with a change in a spiritual sense. A very warm, positive feeling, the sense of optimism which wasn't there an hour before.'
Orientated towards the future	'There was a change in the way I viewed the future. I can say that looking back now.'
Highly personalized to each individual.	'I know the client is becoming more hopeful when she can say "Maybe its ok for me to be happy".'

provided by the interviewees, in particular, the ex-clients, we can see signs of increased hope in the ex-clients as the therapy progressed (Table 2.1 on the previous page).

Thus, I can state, with a degree of empirical confidence, that clients do appear to have increased hope as a result of the means identified in this book. Additional empirical quantitative evidence, however, would strengthen (or possibly refute) the theory.

A radical change in practice needed?

At the risk of stating the obvious, all the data I collected from practitioners were obtained from therapists who were currently practising. Such a sampling approach not only lends credibility to the fit and 'grab' of the theory, but also indicates that the theory was implicit in the current, contemporary practice of some bereavement counsellors. Furthermore, this study also shows ample evidence of the value of hope inspiration. However, at the same time there was a complete absence of any theory in the literature which indicated (if and) how bereavement counsellors inspired hope.

Hence, I am left wondering: does this represent something of a paradox? Practitioners clearly need to be aware of the value and theory of hope inspiration, yet it also needs to remain implicit, rather than conscious and explicit.

In response, I would argue that this is not paradoxical. Epistemologists have often argued that all practice has theory present, whether it is implicit or explicit. Whilst some practitioners may feel that some theory may be regarded as removed or distant from the 'real world' of clinical practice, it has been argued that *all* healthcare practice is underpinned by theory (McKenna 1997). Indeed, in his seminal work, Kuhn (1962) declared that theory, be it explicit or implicit, plays a key role in understanding any behaviour, and that there is nothing so useful as a good theory. The practice of bereavement counsellors can be driven by and underpinned by theory, even though the theory remains inherent and embedded.

For example, as a counsellor who often works in a 'person-centred' manner, I am aware of Rogers' (1952) theory of the core conditions. I try to ensure that they are present in my practice, and I try to convey a sense of these core conditions to the client. However, I do not consciously think

'Right, in response to what client X has just said, I need to demonstrate that I empathize,'

or

'In response to what client Y has just told me, I need to tell them overtly, that I do not judge or condemn then.'

Thus, the theory is present, it is having an influence, it is underpinning practice, but it is not overt.

Similarly, just as the interviewees in this study who use Rogers' (1952) person-centred approach to counselling would not be overt in saying

'I'm a warm person, I accept you.'

They would similarly not overtly say,

'I am a hopeful person. There is hope for you. You can become more hopeful.'

Thus, again, the theory is present, it is having an influence, it is underpinning practice, but it is not overt. That is exactly the same situation in which bereavement counsellors can find themselves with regard to the inspiration of hope: aware of the theory; with the theory underpinning and influencing their practice, without the theory being overt.

So, the straightforward answer is 'No – there is no need for a radical change in practice'. However, given the absence of existing theoretical or empirical work within the literature, there is a clear need for increased awareness of the role and value of hope inspiration and, concomitantly, there is a need to be aware of the attitudes and practices that might be seen to be hope-hindering.

Such attitudes and practices include the following: not listening or understanding and not making any effort to communicate the sense that one is listening and trying to understand. Being indifferent, communicating a sense that one does not really care. Lacking a sense of commitment to the person, the process and the potential for hope to re-emerge. Judging the client and expecting him/her to be better, different or to be making more or faster progress. Expecting the person to fit to models of bereavement and arbitrary time frames for recovery from bereavement. Being uncomfortable with the expression of emotion, particularly painful emotions. Expecting the sessions to move at the pace set by the practitioner rather than the client, or worse still, working to the organisation's pace (i.e. expecting recovery within a set number of sessions). Being too prescriptive or practitioner centred. Colluding with the client's sense of hopelessness. Hope hindering attitudes include: being cold and/or indifferent – lacking a sense of genuine care and compassion for the person's well-being, being unempathic or insensitive, lacking a sense of warmth, thus being cold and dispassionate, being judgemental and condemning.

While there is no indication that a radical change in practice is called for, there is nevertheless a need for a subtle shift in practice in order to 'make room' for the additional awareness. This subtle shift includes: ensuring that the rudamentaries, the foundations of hope inspiration are in place first before one moves onto using the particularised hope-inspiring interventions. Ensure that one's bereavement counselling practice is underpinned by the presence of certain hope-inspiring qualities and recognize that these are necessary irrespective of one's theoretical orientation. Focus on 'ways of being' rather than 'ways of doing'. Focus on the interpersonal dynamics and processes between the client and the counsellor rather than the intrapersonal tasks and processes of the client. Be less anxious to fix and 'make it right' and be aware that sometimes clients need to fall apart.

Furthermore, perhaps an increased awareness of the role and value of hope would facilitate another linked shift in practice; namely, focusing less on addressing intrapersonal dynamics within the client, and more on interpersonal dynamics within the bereavement counselling. It would make a lot of sense if training/preparation of grief therapists included this theory, thereby focusing on the inspiration of hope as a result of the relationship established, in addition to the techniques and interventions that are aimed at identifying conflicts of separation.

Freeing rather than fixing

My research shows that hope appears to be inspired as a result of clients feeling free enough to discharge their painful emotions. According to the data obtained from both the counsellors and ex-clients, the presence of such painful feelings within clients can hold them in a position of relative hopelessness. Fixed in the past, dwelling on what was, their pain is a constant reminder of what used to be, of what they have lost, that their hopes were dashed. Thus, there appears to be great potential for hope inspiration in facilitating freedom from such a position. Furthermore, the interviewees spoke of the hope-inspiring value of being able to say negative things about the deceased without feeling judged. They experienced a permissive environment where the expression of such thoughts and feelings did not exacerbate their perception of hopelessness. One ex-client described how, prior to entering into bereavement counselling, she was reluctant to say exactly what she felt, since on the few occasions she had done this, she felt guilty afterwards and the guilt added to her sense of hopelessness. When she then encountered the environment in the counselling, where there was an absence of guilt, blame or judgement, she learned to internalize this acceptance of her own feelings and realized that having such feelings was not uncommon – again indicating the great potential for hope inspiration in facilitating such freedom.

There are two different, but related, forms of freeing: freeing the client to engage in some form of emotional discharge (catharsis), and freeing the client to talk in any way he or she feels the need to. However, some (novice) counsellors may have a belief that the client expects the counsellor to solve or 'fix' his problems (see Chapter 3). Such situations can be exacerbated if the counsellor has to work under the largely artificial pressure of 'waiting lists', 'outcome targets' and a fixed number of sessions. Facilitating or actively encouraging the client to access and express painful emotion or, to rephrase, encouraging the client to 'let go' and 'fall apart', can feel far from fixing the client's problem(s).

It needs to be recognized that, for some counsellors, this focus on 'freeing' rather than containing can be difficult. Such a difficulty is perhaps more often (though not exclusively) associated with inexperienced counsellors. Yet, as this study has highlighted, there is a need to allow people to 'fall apart' in a supportive, non-restrictive environment; to throw off the 'shackles' of previous restrictive and disabling relationships in order that they might gain hope as a result of expressing their painful emotions. Thus it is worth reiterating that there is a clear need for practitioners to be comfortable with the free expression of emotion.

3

Putting the Theory into Practice

Is the theory robust?

The emerging theory indicates that clients who feel their counsellors care about them and with them, simultaneously inspire hope in them too. Similarly, as we have seen, current theory and research literature also indicates that nurses who care about their clients simultaneously inspire hope. Furthermore, the theory and literature indicate that caring and hope appear to be interwoven concepts. Counsellors who 'help' their clients can be seen to 'care' about these clients and a product of this is the implicit inspiration of hope.

In addition, both the emerging theory and the literature show that clients have hope inspired in them by carers who they feel support them (counsellors in the theory, nurses in the literature), help them reflect (on positive memories) and use appropriate touch. Furthermore, within the literature hope is identified as a dynamic concept that fluctuates over time – a life-sustaining force that perhaps remains implicit until the person is in need of hope (e.g. Dufault and Martocchio 1985; Farran, Salloway and Clark 1990; Lynch 1965). In the same way the emerging theory in this book indicates that hope inspiration is an implicit process, yet unequivocally bound up with the totality of the bereavement counselling process.

Not all the methods, interventions or ways of hope inspiration that I will identify in this book are echoed in the literature. For example, within the first sub-core variable (*Forging the connection and relationship*, see Chapter 4) the following processes described by the interviewees can be viewed as hope-inspiring:

- counsellors passing the implicit tests set by the clients
- clients learning that they can express their feelings and talk about the loss without destroying someone else
- counsellors not 'running away' from the client's 'dark side', the expression of really raw emotion/material
- the formation of a new significant relationship.

Within the second sub-core variable (*Facilitating a cathartic release*) the following processes were described by clients and counsellors as hope-inspiring:

- the freedom to talk about the deceased in whatever ways the clients needed to
- the considered, purposeful use of silence
- counsellors not colluding with the client's perceived sense of hopelessness.

Within the third sub-core variable (*Experiencing a healthy [good] ending*) the following processes were described as hope-inspiring:

- accomplishing certain tasks of grieving
- clients avoiding a repeat of previous restricted or learned responses to loss.

Similarly, all the ways or methods identified within the literature were not also indicated within the emerging theory. For example, the methods or ways of hope inspiration titled 'spiritual strategies' and 'mental attitude of determinism' (Miller 1989), and lightheartedness (Herth 1990) were not identified in the emerging theory in my research.

What this apparent disparity perhaps begins to suggest is that there may be central rudiments of the basic social process of hope inspiration which appear to transcend substantive areas and have value and applicability throughout the formal area of healthcare relationships between practitioner and service user. While I would not wish to seem to uphold a philosophical view that contends that there is only one unique reality, perhaps the evidence of these shared, inter-subjective meanings indicates that the process described in this theory may resonate with the realities of many different groups of people and may thus have credibility within these world views.

Examination of the commonalities between the emerging theory and the current literature indicates that, for the most part, the commonalities describe the role of human qualities, ways of being, the presence and importance of implicit hope within the practitioner and the nurturing or helping environment (Cutcliffe 1995; Cutcliffe and Grant 2001; Herth 1990; Miller 1989; Vaillot 1970). By contrast, examination of the differences in the processes of hope inspiration suggests that, in addition to having these rudiments, idiosyncratic to each substantive area (e.g. Oncology, HIV/AIDS, Coronary care, Bereavement Counselling), each substantive area has its own set of particularised interventions. From this it is reasonable to postulate that the rudimentaries act as the foundation, the building blocks, upon which further interventions are built.

Consequently, one implication for bereavement counselling practice becomes apparent: the importance of first establishing or setting in place the rudimentaries and, following this, using the particularised interventions identified in this book which are idiosyncratic to the substantive area. It may even be that on some occasions, or for some people, the rudimentaries alone may be sufficient as a means of inspiring hope; however, the particularised interventions are unlikely to be enough on their own. Moreover, it is unlikely that the effective counsellor will move straight into using the particularised interventions, without first ensuring that the rudimentaries, the foundations for hope inspiration, are established.

Do different approaches to counselling affect the basic social process of hope inspiration?

Data were collected for my study from counsellors who used a psychodynamic (psychoanalytical), humanistic (person-centred), gestalt, or an eclectic approach to counselling. The philosophical underpinnings and resultant ways of working of each of these approaches share some similarities, but also show clear differences (e.g. the temporal focus of the therapy, the use of interventions or focusing on the core conditions within the therapy, the degree of challenge or confrontation within the therapy).

Whilst acknowledging that differences in these approaches existed, one further commonality discovered appeared to be the processes of hope inspiration within bereavement counselling. Irrespective of the particular theoretical approach(es) that underpinned the counsellors' ways of working, the basic social process of hope inspiration appeared to be fundamentally the same: that is, it remained subtle, unobtrusive and bound up with the therapy.

There existed slight differences in the way certain interventions were used as a subtle means of hope inspiration. For example, the therapist or counsellor who predominantly used a gestalt approach would perhaps be more prompt to challenge some of the client's limiting, restrictive attitudes and behaviours. The counsellor or therapist who used a psycho-dynamic approach predominantly would perhaps be more swift to explore how earlier experiences of loss and hopelessness were affecting the current experience of loss and hopelessness. The counsellor or therapist who used a humanistic approach predominantly would perhaps be more concerned with focusing on the use of the core conditions of warmth, empathy, genuineness and unconditional positive regard. Nevertheless, none of the counsellors made reference to any explicit attempts to inspire or project hope. Indeed, such overt projection was viewed as damaging and destructive – an imposition of the counsellor or therapist's view (and hope) onto the client. However, all the counsellors made reference to the presence of hope within themselves and within the counselling process; to the re-emergence of hope within the client as the counselling process (or therapy) continued; to the hopeful atmosphere created and to the hopeful views/beliefs of the person and of the process of counselling.

It is perhaps important to acknowledge this argument, as it illustrates that hope inspiration appeared to be achieved more as a result of the presence of certain qualities in the counsellor or therapist, and the application of such qualities, rather than as a result of sophisticated techniques. As indicated in the literature review, and supported by my research findings, bereavement counselling for individuals experiencing a complicated grief reaction appears to require a particular interpersonal environment or atmosphere. Rogers (1952) is perhaps most noted for suggesting the necessary and sufficient conditions that make up such an interpersonal counselling environment. Therefore, given the similarities between Rogers' (1952) theory and the theory induced in this book, a question that should be asked and addressed is: how is the theory of hope inspiration different from, or adding to, Rogers' theory of the necessary and sufficient conditions within therapy?

In response to this question, the theory induced in this book builds upon the central tenets of Rogers' theory and posits that there may be another necessary and sufficient core condition in bereavement counselling, and that would be the core condition of hope/hopefulness. Just as a therapist or counsellor using Rogers' person-centred approach to counselling would be concerned with demonstrating and communicating warmth, empathy, genuineness, and unconditional positive regard, the bereavement counsellors in this study were equally concerned with demonstrating and communicating hope and hopefulness. In the same way that a therapist using Rogers' person-centred approach to counselling would not be overt in saying, 'I'm a warm person, I empathise with you, and I accept you', the bereavement counsellors in this study did not overtly say, 'I am a hopeful person. There is hope for you. You can become more hopeful.'

The theory appears to indicate that, without the inspiration of hope, the bereavement counselling would be missing a vital element. If the counsellors fail to bring this hope into the therapy environment, a key resource required by the client is not present and the client cannot replenish their depleted hope resource. The literature review indicated that the complete absence of hope in the individual leads to his/her eventual demise. Bereavement counselling without the presence and influence of hope can, therefore, be seen to lead to an exacerbation of the client's hopeless state.

If this argument is accepted, there are major implications for practice – and theory, education and training). Current literature in the substantive area of grief therapy (e.g. Lendrum and Syme 1992; Worden 1991) appears to have a significant focus on tasks and techniques. In his chapter, 'Grief Therapy: Resolving Pathological Grief' Worden (1991) suggests the goals of therapy are:

> to identify and resolve the conflicts of separation which preclude the completion of the mourning tasks. (pp.79–80)

Similarly, Lendrum and Syme (1992) suggest:

> The counsellor's task is to recognize the protection and its function without colluding in the denial of the avoided feeling. (p.150)

Whilst less attention is given to it, both authors do make reference to the relationship between client and counsellor. However, the emphasis is clearly on addressing intrapersonal dynamics within the client, not on interpersonal dynamics within the counselling. Yet, if hope/hopefulness is considered as a further necessary and sufficient core condition, the theory of grief therapy needs to reflect this finding and, more important, to acknowledge that, whilst some inspiration of hope does appear to occur as a result of specific interventions (e.g. identifying and addressing conflicts of separation), the essence of hope inspiration appears to reside in the caring, interpersonal relationship. Consequently, the resulting training/preparation of grief counsellors and therapists needs to include this theory, which focuses on the inspiration of hope as a result of the relationship established, in addition to the techniques and interventions which are aimed at identifying conflicts of separation. This argument is examined in more detail in further discussion points.

How do practitioners maintain their own hope levels?

My findings indicate that the person responsible for bringing hope into the therapy is the counsellor or therapist. Furthermore, the therapist's hope is vital to the inspiration of hope within the client, since the therapist, through the process of emotional and spiritual projection, projects his/her own hope into the client and the therapy environment. As a result of this it becomes evident that, in order for hope to be projected from the therapist into the client, it is incumbent for practitioners to maintain their own hope levels.

Personal hope is not a limitless resource. Lynch (1965) has argued that hope cannot sustain the individual indefinitely, particularly when that individual's hope is being used to feed and support itself. Consequently, given that hope cannot sustain one person indefinitely, it is reasonable to suggest that hope cannot similarly sustain two people indefinitely. Moreover, if one person's hope is being used to sustain two people (in this instance the therapist's hope is sustaining both the client and the therapist), then the hope resource is likely to be depleted more quickly than if it was sustaining only one person. Additionally, clients experiencing a complicated grief reaction and requiring bereavement counselling have been identified as being in particular need of hope. Thus, their implicit demands made on the therapist's hope are likely to be substantial. It becomes evident, therefore, that the demands made on the therapist's hope as he/she engages in bereavement counselling are considerable.

In the same way that the germ or seed of hope still present in these clients looks to the outside world and seeks help, and finds this in the form of the therapist, the hope within the therapist also looks to the world outside and finds help in the form of clinical supervision. The counsellors and therapists in this study indicated that the principal method of ensuring that they maintained their own hope was through the clinical supervision they received. If the counsellors do not continue receiving clinical supervision, then it follows logically that eventually they will reach a point where they can no longer inspire hope, and may thus no longer be able to provide effective bereavement counselling.

Are there differences between novice and expert counsellors' attempts at hope inspiration?

All the counsellors and therapists who provided data for the research might be categorized as 'veteran' or highly experienced. Whilst the counsellors themselves may feel a little uncomfortable with the title 'expert', they do fit the criteria for expert status identified in Patricia Benner's 1984 seminal work.

A common feature of relatively inexperienced or novice counsellors is perhaps a desire to 'fix' things. Speaking of her personal experiences of receiving therapy for many years Bobbie Kerr states,

> the first thing you have to learn is to identify the problems. Once you are able to do that, much later, you can learn how to work out practical ways of resolving these problems. (Barker and Kerr 2001, pp.38–9)

Consequently, it is not entirely surprising that novice counsellors may entertain a belief that the client expects them to solve or fix these problems. Similarly, if the client has a problem concerning his or her sense of hopelessness, or lack of hope, then it is likely that novice counsellors may want to 'fix' this lack of hope. Although such beliefs may be based on the highest motives, they may yet, where the inspiration of hope is concerned, prove counterproductive.

In wanting to be seen to be doing, to be making a difference, and anxious perhaps to convince the client of their good intentions and their skill, the novice counsellor may be too hasty in trying to 'make it right'. He or she can be too quick to suggest that hope still exists; that the future can be a hopeful one. Rather than allowing these perceptions to evolve during the process of the therapy as a product of the client–therapist relationship, the novice counsellor tries to force the issue; to force hope.

By contrast, the expert counsellors encourage and allow the hope to emerge. This difference was captured early on in the data collection in which counsellors made such statements as

> I didn't focus on inspiring or instilling hope, it was bound up, implicit.

> I project my hope into the situation at a very basic or fundamental level just by my willingness to work with the client.

The subtle, unobtrusive nature of hope inspiration within bereavement counselling (and its association with stillness) would perhaps be difficult for novices to accept. When I was a novice myself, in various domains of practice (including bereavement work), I was anxious to be seen to be helping and this was perhaps counterproductive.

As novices we sometimes need certainty, 'check lists' we can follow to guide our practice. As novices we also sometimes need to follow a series of tasks, or interventions, ideally a list of evidence-based interventions. Thus, in the context of hope inspiration in bereavement counselling, novices sometimes need a sense of: if we do X, Y and Z, if we follow the step-by-step process, we can thus inspire hope. Yet, the 'check list' approach to hope inspiration is likely to have a very limited value in bereavement counselling, particularly given the arguments described earlier in this chapter.

There is another pressure that novice bereavement counsellors may feel and which may influence their attempts to inspire hope: the current 'drivers' of healthcare. It is reasonable to say that contemporary healthcare is increasingly driven by two factors: the need for cost-effectiveness and the need for evidence-based practice. Consequently, novice bereavement counsellors may well have both a desire and a duty (to the organisation) to ensure that as much of their practice as possible is both cost-effective and evidence-based. There is a similar, concomitant 'pressure' on such practitioners to demonstrate that their practice is making a difference. Such overt, highly visible practice lends itself to audit and quantitative research wherein their evidence base can be established, and some attempt made to determine their cost-effectiveness.

On the other hand, the emerging theory described in this book suggests that implicit and subtle methods exist in addition to explicit ones. Indeed, the inspiration of hope needs to remain implicit. Furthermore, such implicit 'interventions' are less visible or tangible, and often have no immediate 'product'. They are thus less amenable to audit or deductive research, and similarly would present inherent methodological difficulties to someone wishing to determine their cost-effectiveness. It is reasonable, therefore, to postulate that such practices might be deemed to be less valuable by novice bereavement counsellors who feel the need to demonstrate the value and worth of their practice. As a result, the novice practitioner is ushered into more 'overt' attempts to inspire hope and thus, ironically, becomes less effective.

Is there a broader impact on mental health nursing?

This question is bound up with the debate concerning the proper focus of mental health nursing. The suggestion is that the inspiration of hope can be seen to represent further evidence of the need to return to a more human-focused model of mental health nursing.

Views of mental health nursing can currently be separated into two polarized groups and Dr Liam Clarke provides a useful summary of these. According to Clarke (1999) the first group believe they have the answers to most of the big questions in mental health nursing (and healthcare for that matter). They believe the physical sciences offer up these answers or are on the cusp of solving whatever remains. Behavioral and cognitive sciences are seen by this group as having produced a workable range of cognitive and socially focused interventions.

The second group, suggests Clarke (1999), believe that the search for the answers in mental health nursing has only begun. He states:

It's not that they see biological discoveries as unworthy; it is simply that they are inappropriate questions for nurses. (p.75)

Barker (1999a) offers similar conclusions, suggesting that, whilst technology may offer intriguing insights into what appears to be happening on a biological level, it tells us little or nothing about the human experience of mental illness. Belonging firmly to this second group of people, Barker (1999a) stands on the shoulders of those before him, namely Sullivan, Peplau, Altschul and Szasz when suggesting:

I see nursing as primarily a developmental activity: nurses provide the conditions under which people can grow and develop. (p.70)

Such a position appears to have much in common with Nightingale's (1859) axiom that nurses do not heal anyone; nurses place people in the best position possible in order to let nature heal them. Perhaps a brief etymology of the word 'nursing' may also shed some light on what can be regarded as the proper focus of nursing. 'Nursing' is an expression based on the old French word *norrice* or *nourrice* meaning 'to nourish'. If nurses do not nourish – in all ways – the person who is patient, employing the kind of 'nurturance' referred to in other posting, then it is questionable whether the activity can truly be called 'nursing' (Barker 1999a).

Additional authors have attempted to unravel and discover the proper focus or nature of mental health nursing. Hill and Michael (1996) use a phenomenological approach to uncover the meaning of psychiatric/ mental (P/MH) health nurses' 'concrete activity'. Their initial findings indicate that the core activity is working with extraordinary people within 'ordinary' relationships and in ordinary contexts. They acknowledge that these findings offer only a tentative understanding and that, consequently, psychiatric nurses have a moral and ethical duty to make every effort to define and describe such skills, no matter how difficult this may prove. Chambers (1998) makes similar remarks, suggesting that P/MH nurses must demonstrate ordinariness and humanness through their verbal and non-verbal behaviour.

Hill and Michael (1996) state that the 'craft' of P/MH nursing often gets overlooked. They argue that one element of this uniqueness is in the psychiatric nurses' skill in attempting to give all types of relationship an ordinary context: this is an integral part of our craft of care and a core activity. They assert that such nurses focus on ordinary contact that is respectful and empathic.

Similarly, as a result of a collaborative inquiry, Barker, Reynolds and Stevenson (1997) maintain that, since P/MH nursing is primarily concerned with establishing the conditions necessary for promoting the person's unique growth and development:

> Developing an effective relationship with people in care must be a primary concern for all nurses, but should have a more specific concern in psychiatric nursing. (p.666)

The argument that mental health care needs to return to a more human focus is not limited to British academics. Writing from his experiences as a survivor of the Holocaust and as a therapist, Frankl (1959) subscribes to the need for a more human focus to mental health care. He argues that there is a need for psychiatry to be re-humanized. He states:

> For too long a time, for half a century in fact, psychiatry tried to interpret the human mind merely as a mechanism, and consequently the therapy of mental disease merely in terms of technique. (p.156)

Having identified that there is a significant body of knowledge that emphasizes the need for a human-focused model of mental health care, it is worth considering how the inspiration of hope theory contributes to this body of knowledge. The theory indicates that the inspiration of hope is bound up with the formation of a connection and a relationship between the client and counsellor; with counsellors' 'caring with' and 'caring about' the client; with the presence and influence of the inter-personal and intrapersonal conditions, with counsellors' demonstration of an unconditional acceptance and understanding, listening and hearing the client, and removing any sense of coercion of psychological pressure; and, finally, with establishing the human–human connection, and the projection of hope and hopefulness from the counsellor to the client, through the spiritual connection.

Consequently, this theory suggests that the inspiration of hope is bound up with the human-focused model of mental health care and not with neurobiology, or models that consider the mind to be little more than a physical brain in need of a chemical solutions to its problems, or those that stress reductionalist techniques.

4

Forging the Connection and Relationship

In this chapter, I provide a detailed description of the processes and interventions that the bereavement counsellor can use to inspire hope in the sub-core variable indentified as 'forging the connection and relationship'.[1]

This phase of the bereavement counselling encounter is concerned with the basic psychosocial processes of the formation of a relationship between the client and the counsellor, and testing and trusting as a means to facilitate relationship formation. It is concerned with the engagement of the client and the establishment of a connection between the counsellor and client. While the uniqueness of the process of establishing each relationship needs to be recognized, the counsellors did describe certain attitudes, qualities, skills and interventions that they possessed and utilized in order to enhance the formation of this relationship. That is not to say that the presence or utilization of such phenomena meant that the counsellors had a mechanistic approach to relationship formation. Indeed, to adopt such a 'synthetic' approach, or to follow a 'formula' was regarded as, not only counterproductive, but as an anathema to the philosophical underpinnings of many of the counsellors.

---

1   For a detailed summary of my grounded theory research process, see Appendix I.

Experiencing a caring, human–human connection

As indicated in table A.6, this sub-core variable has five broad categories of interventions and processes. The first category 'Experiencing a caring, human-human connection' appears to have three properties. First, there is a property that is concerned with counsellors caring about and with the client. Second, there is a property that is concerned with the human–human connection between the client and counsellor. The third property is concerned with the bereaved client's experience of re-engaging in a meaningful relationship.

Counsellors caring about the client

The counsellors stressed the importance of setting in place the intra- and interpersonal conditions necessary for hope to be nurtured. The counsellors wished to create the interpersonal environment where the clients would feel 'cared about' and consequently counsellors focused on 'ways of being' as opposed to 'doing'. Such caring practice was concerned with demonstrating an unconditional acceptance and understanding, listening and hearing the client, and removing any sense of coercion of psychological pressure. Importantly, the presence of these qualities alone in the counsellor would not be enough for hope to be nurtured in the client. The qualities also have to be conveyed or demonstrated, and need to be genuine. The interviewees described this in the following ways:

> When people feel they are being understood, when they feel they are being listened to and not being judged, then this will make the person more hopeful. (Int. 8).

> We remove the psychological pressure, and thus allow the hope to emerge, by the use of natural, normal (Rogerian) core conditions, which help the person to feel that they are not under any pressure. (Int. 8).

> Bound up with the importance of really hearing clients at the start of therapy, is actively accepting that where they are is completely normal and understandable. (Int. 7).

This theory of hope inspiration indicates that to experience unconditional acceptance is hope inspiring. The ex-clients described this in the following ways:

> I was convinced and assured that my therapist was hearing me, hearing my story, when I noticed he had watery eyes. (Int. 11).

> I got a sense that my therapist cares about me. If I hadn't got that sense then I wouldn't have gone to see him. No way. (Int. 10).

> As a result of sensing or experiencing my therapist hearing me, it was one of the most mentally healthy times in my life. (Int. 11).

> The way the counsellor made me feel supported, the most marked thing was, whatever it was that I said, however irrational that seemed or however unreasonable that seemed, that was ok. It was accepted. (Int. 9).

> Experiencing that affirmation gave me the sense of, 'feel what you need to feel, do what you need to do' and then I can move onto the next stage. And I knew that the next time the pain grabs me, then actually it's all right. It's nothing to be too scared about, I know it will pass. (Int. 10).

These messages of care and acceptance counteract the prohibitive, restrictive messages from (some of) the significant others in the client's life. To be told, implicitly or explicitly, 'what you are feeling or experiencing is wrong' leads to a perception of self that is negative, and only serves to perpetuate the sense of hopelessness. Consequently, there appears to be a substantial potential for the inspiration of hope in messages of care and acceptance contrary to prohibitive and restrictive messages. The counsellors could be said to have communicated messages such as:

> What you are feeling is entirely understandable, appropriate and ok.

> It may well even be necessary for you to experience such feelings in order for you to resolve this.

> You have the potential to negotiate this experience and grow from it.

When this happened this gradually shifted the clients' position to a more hopeful one. Instead of feeling hopeless and having thoughts centered on hopelessness, the clients were left thinking and feeling more hopeful. The ex-clients described this in the following ways:

> Having one's feelings, one's anger accepted by the therapist helps with part of that process moving from despair to hope. (Int. 11).

> When I felt affirmed by the therapist I started to believe that I am not going to go mad, that I am not going to stay in this place forever. (Int. 10).

> Part of the value of being able to express emotion is that it is acknowledged, validated. (Int. 9).

Thus data provided by the interviewees suggests that this interpersonal climate is precisely the atmosphere that is required for the nurturing and inspiration of hope. The qualitative data indicate that for a client to feel that somebody else cares about them and their situation, that somebody else feels they are valuable and worthwhile, that somebody else cares enough to be concerned about their well-being even though the client may not care, is hope inspiring.

The human–human connection between client and counsellor

Second, it may appear somewhat simplistic and obvious, yet it is worth emphasizing that there is a great deal of therapeutic potential, and with that, potential for hope inspiration, in establishing the very fundamental, potentially powerful human–human connection. Some of this human connection involved the counsellor communicating to the client that whatever the client is experiencing is ok with the counsellor; that there is no one universally 'correct' response to bereavement; and that what clients are experiencing, whatever that is, is completely 'normal' and understandable. As a result of the counsellor really hearing and accepting the client, a connection is established between them. This aspect of hope inspiration occurred at a very fundamental level of human existence. People need to engage and connect with other people. If this engagement is present then the outcome is another fundamental aspect of our existence, hope. If this connection is absent, if the client feels isolated, alone, abandoned, then the outcome will be continued hopelessness.

The interviewees described this in the following ways:

The making of the relationship is in itself hope inspiring. (Int. 7).

It just felt enormously healing for her just to share that with someone. (Int. 7).

Similarly, the ex-clients indicated the importance and primacy of this human–human connection and how hope inspiring this connection was. Not only did it need to be present, otherwise the therapy and inspiration of hope wouldn't occur. But additionally, the human-human connection needed to be established early on in the process. The ex-clients described this in the following ways:

The therapist can plant a bit of hope by communicating that he/she cares, that I am not alone, isolated in this. (Int. 11).

But I suppose that their (the therapist's) connectedness with me perhaps helps me connect with something inside to stop myself going into destruction. (Int. 10).

The bereaved client's experience of re-engaging in a meaningful relationship

Third, this human–human connection may be even more relevant and powerful for this particular client group. As indicated in Chapter 2, many clients who have experienced and not resolved a 'complicated bereavement', have a need to invest in another meaningful relationship. Such re-engagement is evidence of the client re-investing in life (Worden 1988). Therefore, when clients form this human connection with their counsellor, then maybe these clients begin to realize that they can be in another close relationship. They begin to internalize that this human connection is not a betrayal of the memory of the deceased; that they can exist in such relationships without feeling that they are being unfaithful or experiencing intense feelings of guilt. Clients can then begin to internalize the feelings of acceptance without feeling guilty. In addition, this human connection helps the client realize that they can form another intimate relationship, that they are still capable of doing so. This relationship shows the clients that they have a future, that all is not lost, that they can be intimate again, that someone believes in them as a person, believes they have potential, believes they are worth the time and effort. One outcome of each of these realizations is an increased sense of hope and hopefulness, and similarly, feelings contrary to their feelings of hopelessness. The interviewees described this in the following ways:

> If someone is really fixed in their restrictive constructs, then no matter how many times you say, 'It's not your fault' they don't want to hear you because their guilt is very important to them. It is also their way of hanging onto the person. (Int. 7).

> When clients start to internalize the acceptance that I offer, then they become more accepting of themselves. (Int. 7).

The ex-clients echoed the value and importance of this new relationship. They described how such a new relationship was often dissimilar to the prohibitive relationships they encountered elsewhere, and that within this enabling, accepting, new relationship with the therapist, they experienced a new sense of freedom. The ex-clients described this in the following ways:

> If I didn't get a sense of acceptance from my therapist, that would have made me feel very alone. (Int. 11).

> When we did engage with one another, I found that what I was feeling was ok. (Int. 10).

> It really felt like being known and having some understanding of what this might be like for me. Interested and supportive through and through. (Int. 11).

Countering the projections of hopelessness

The second category I identified 'Countering the projections of hopelessness' appears to have two properties, one concerned with the clients' conscious or unconscious expectations that the counsellor will not pass the tests, and a second property that is concerned with the clients' thoughts that any disclosure from them could harm somebody else.

Client's test-setting for the counsellors

Given that clients set certain tests within the therapy (consciously or subconsciously) from their position of relative hopelessness, there is likely to be a projected expectation that the tests will not be passed. The clients' hopelessness is not limited to his/her person but is also projected into how he/she perceives and encounters the world. Hence if a client is expecting the counsellor to fail the test, the hope inspiring value of not failing this test becomes evident. The counsellor reacts to the test in a way that does not fit the client's perception of hopelessness. The counsellor's resulting behaviour offers a subliminal message of: 'All is not hopeless. You expected me to fail and thus reinforce your beliefs that there is no hope, but I have not done this. I have responded in a way that suggests to you that there is hope.'

The interviewees expressed this in the following ways:

> The testing out of the counsellor can occur at a subconscious level. (Int. 8).

> When clients are talking about things that are painful, then they are observing you as much as you are observing them. Consequently, they will pick up on the non-verbal points on whether you are really listening to them. (Int. 8).

> When I expressed anger in my past relationships, my mother emotionally distanced herself from me. Thus I learned to conform and not be a naughty boy. Consequently, I expected that when I expressed anger in the therapy, the therapist would withdraw from me too. But she didn't, she heard my pain (Int. 12).

Clients realising they do not need to fear hurting others

The second property indicates that as a result of the client beginning to test out the counsellor by giving vent to some of his/her pain, the client begins to see that he/she can express these thoughts and feelings without destroying somebody else. The interviewees expressed this in the following ways:

> It is very important that the counsellor doesn't psychologically 'run away' from the expression of pain. (Int. 8).

Clients sometimes have fantasies that they were somehow responsible for the loss of their loved one and these fantasies are projected into the therapy. The client can even fantasize that if they share their thoughts and feelings about their experience, that the counsellor will be the next person to be harmed. For example, the interviewees stated:

> What I find is that clients sometimes protect me, protect me from something that has horrified them. (Int. 7).

> Clients don't want to upset you, and they wonder, 'Can you be strong enough for me?' (Int. 4).

Thus, the realization that counsellors are not being damaged or harmed by what the client is telling them has a two fold value. It starts to challenge and dispel, albeit implicitly, the client's belief or fantasy that they were responsible for the death of the deceased. Additionally, it demonstrates to the client that they can give vent to these thoughts and feelings without harming anyone. Perhaps the most significant message and subsequent benefit the response of the counsellor to such disclosures is the following. The client can begin to internalize that if the counsellor can hear, feel and experience the disclosure of the pain, or the dark side, without being destroyed by this, then maybe the client can hear, feel and experience this disclosure for him- or herself and equally not be destroyed by it.

In this realization lies the potential for the emergence of hope. Due to his/her sense (and projection) of hopelessness, it is unlikely that the client ever imagined or hoped that he/she would be able to ventilate all his/her repressed pain. Since these clients are 'stuck' in the bereavement process, this pain and emotional discomfort may have been ever present for the client since the loss of his/her loved one. Consequently, for the counsellor to pass the test; for the counsellor to hear, feel and experience this dark side and not be damaged by it, is to challenge this sense of hopelessness and resulting negative thoughts. The ex-clients expressed this in the following ways:

> At times, I felt a distinct sense of the therapist's tenacity and commitment. Committed to me. (Int. 11).

> The therapist communicated her tenacity and commitment by not being too obsessive or inflexible about when I see her. (Int. 9).

> The therapist wouldn't let me throw in the towel. (Int. 11).

Unwavering commitment

The third category, 'Unwavering commitment' is concerned with the process and operationalisation of the therapist's tenacity, commitment and covenant. One test that is common within bereavement counselling, involves the client opening up, showing something of his/her 'dark side' and the counsellor does not run away from this disclosure. This test is particularly important in bereavement counselling because part of the healing process (and hope inspiring process) that many clients appear to benefit from is accessing their pain and giving vent to their emotions in order to discharge this pain (see Chapter 8). However, this emotional release is unlikely to happen unless the client feels safe. Consequently, clients need to establish that they can vent these painful emotions. They determine whether or not it is safe to do so by showing a glimpse of their pain; a glimpse of the intensity of emotion or 'horror' of the situation. In response to this disclosure, it is necessary for the counsellor to demonstrate that they are not damaged by it. That they can not only tolerate it but furthermore can accept whatever the client chooses to disclose.

The fact that the counsellor does not abandon the client as a result of this disclosure is thus hope inspiring. It is hope inspiring for clients to see that the counsellor can hear whatever the client needs to say and will not retreat or withdraw from it. Clients who have experienced a complicated bereavement reaction are likely to have a particular fear of being abandoned again (as they were 'abandoned' by the deceased). Accordingly, the hope inspiring potential of a counsellor communicating to the client that they will not abandon them, that they have an unwavering commitment too them, no matter what the client brings up, begins to become apparent.

The interviewees expressed this in the following ways:

> The counselling relationship becomes a 'test bed' for the client, for them to discover whether or not they can tolerate talking about their loss, if they can tolerate their pain. (Int. 8).

> Sometimes clients think because they found the bereavement horrific, the counsellor would find it horrific, so how could the counsellor possibly hear it? (Int. 7).

So clients test the counsellor out, test out that they are strong enough, that they will be able to cope with whatever the client brings up. (Int. 4).

She would touch her raw material, dip into it, then withdraw from it again. (Int. 5).

The ex-clients made similar remarks, which indicated that as a result of having to adapt to the expectations of those people around them, they had the implicit expectation that the counselling relationship would be nother prohibitive relationship. This perception is no doubt influenced by their position (and resulting perception) of relative hopelessness. Hence, they were prepared to test the counsellor but expected him/her to fail. The ex-clients described this in the following ways:

The barometer or test of the relationship is measured in terms of, 'How far can I go in terms of feeling what I need to feel?' and 'How far is he prepared to hold me without it being too much for him?' (Int. 10).

I tested him by doing it (showing emotion, experiencing the bereavement) and him not shutting himself off from me, not withdrawing from me. (Int. 10).

When I expressed anger towards my therapist she said, 'I'm not going to go away.' That really touched me, that very powerful feeling of acceptance. (Int. 12).

Rediscovering trust

The fourth category 'Rediscovering trust' is concerned with the processes of testing and trusting. Clients feel the need to test things out in the bereavement counselling. There may well be a testing of the counsellor, the relationship they establish, or an element of testing themselves. These tests are necessary in order to reach a place or establish a sense of trust and yet may well occur outside of the client's consciousness. As a consequence of such tests being 'passed', the counselling environment became a more trusting place. Further, as a result of testing and learning to trust, clients gain hope and become more hopeful. The interviewees described this in the following ways:

> The testing out that occurred is bound up with the process of establishing trust, conveying acceptance. (Int. 5).

> The client has to go through a testing out phase, even get angry with you, before they can access the really raw material. (Int. 2).

> The one important thing (in terms of acceptance, understanding and trust) is that people are allowed to fail. (Int. 6).

> One of the boundaries is that we are clear that we are going to do some serious work in here. (Int. 4).

As a result of the counsellor passing the tests that the client poses, clients learn that they can trust again. Clients come to realize that they can place their trust in another significant individual and that this trust will not be broken. When a person loses a significant other, a common dynamic arising from this loss is a distinct unwillingness to trust again. There is a sense that the deceased has broken the trust that existed between the deceased and the person. When the person has accepted the loss; achieved a resolution, then they can begin to trust again. For individuals who experience a complicated bereavement reaction, this unwillingness to trust again remains present. Due to their sense of hopelessness, they think and feel that they will never be able to trust again. They fear that they will never be able to share the intimacy and reciprocity of trust. Consequently, as the clients begin to realize that they can trust, that they can share this intimacy, that their future holds the potential for interpersonal relationships, then the clients feel more hopeful. The interviewees described this in the following way:

> At that point she was testing the relationship, testing that we could share a closeness. (Int. 5).

Bound up with the clients learning to trust again is the therapist's commitment and tenacity. With each test that that the therapist passes, with each progressive disclosure that doesn't shock or harm the therapist, the client gains a sense of therapist being in the therapy for the duration. As the clients experience these senses they begin to be internalized. The interviewees described this in the following way:

> If I can acknowledge the horror of the event, without being overwhelmed, then it creates a trust. A trust that I am going to stay throughout the whole thing, that I won't run away from it. (Int. 5).

The ex-clients also alluded to this process of learning to trust again through the development of the relationship with the counsellor and thus having to learn to trust the counsellor. The trust that was established was not present at the very beginning of the relationship. However, progressively and throughout the counselling session, the clients gained a sense that the counsellor was trustworthy and learned to trust a significant person once more. The ex-clients expressed this in the following ways:

> I felt that I could trust my therapist because, whilst he could be confrontational, he never pushed me too far. (Int. 11).

> But then I 'sussed' him out as someone I wanted to work with and that was something about being able to trust him. (Int. 10).

Permeating hope throughout the counselling encounter

The final category is concerned with the processes of inspiring hope by and through the blossoming relationship. The presence of the counsellor's hope permeates throughout the relationship. It is communicated implicitly by the therapist's willingness to engage with the client and furthermore, as a by-product of this relationship formation. Since many of the strategies and processes of hope inspiration within this sub-core variable are subtle and unobtrusive, and the processes are implicit, this illustrates something of the integrated nature of the theory. In that this sub-core variable is linked with the implicit projection of hope and hopefulness core variable (see Chapter 1).

A purpose of this sub-core variable is that it sets in place the foundation upon which the other interventions, and thus the potential for hope inspiration, is based. The relationship or engagement between client and counsellor comes first. Without the presence of the relationship, the potential of any other intervention is reduced. Counsellors were eager to point out that while their work with bereft clients contained some specific interventions, e.g. interventions to raise awareness in the client, interventions to challenge defences, early work with clients centered on conveying certain qualities. Consequently, there was no 'magic formula' for establishing a relationship of for inspiring hope, however, attention was given to first creating the interpersonal environment (i.e. engaging and forming a relationship) upon which the remainder of the therapy would be conducted. The interviewees described this in the following ways:

> For the first two or three meetings she told me her story. She was able to tell me her story. (Int. 8).

> The first thing I am doing with clients is really hearing them. (Int. 7).

Similarly, the ex-clients described the necessity of the relationship. How the relationship acted as a foundation. How, without the sense of safety and trust grounded in the relationship, there would be no discharge of painful emotions; there would be no moving forward. Consequently it can be seen that hope inspired as a result of strategies and interventions in phase two and three of this theory, would be limited in their effectiveness without the presence of the connection, the relationship between the client and counsellor. Thus, the fact that the engagement between the client and the counsellor is established first alludes to the sense of stages or phases to the process of hope inspiration. Therefore, perhaps it could be argued that forging the connection, the relationship, in bereavement counselling could be regarded as the beginning of hope new for the client. The ex-clients described this in the following ways:

> I needed the engagement with the therapist and the sense of trust to be present, in order to allow the angry discharges to occur. (Int. 11).

> We spent several months cultivating the trust for the real work. (Int. 11).

> I felt like if I can hold onto this being (this connection/engagement), like an anchor, then their solid point enables me to reach further than if I was just on my own. (Int. 10).

5

Facilitating a Cathartic Release

In this chapter, I provide a detailed description of the processes and interventions that the bereavement counsellor can use to inspire hope in the research sub-core variable 'facilitating a cathartic release'. This phase of the bereavement counselling encounter is concerned with the basic psychosocial processes of enabling and facilitating the release of any painful feelings that the client may have. It involves efforts to create the emotional environment where catharsis is possible.

An integral part of bereavement counselling involves facilitating the release of the client's intensely painful feelings. The data in this study suggests an integral component of hope inspiration within bereavement counselling is this same facilitation and the cathartic release that follows. While it may seem contradictory to suggest that enabling and encouraging someone to access their pain is hope inspiring, it is important to note that it is a cathartic process. Not only is there intense relief in discharging these painful emotions but, until this happens, the client is less able to contemplate a hopeful future (and maybe any future at all). However, it requires a 'leap of faith' on the part of the counsellor in that clients are often resistant to accessing this pain due to its severity and intensity. On occasion, the counsellor may appoint himself or herself, on an unsolicited basis, to challenge and enable this catharsis; believing, hoping and having the faith that it is in the client's best interest to do so. The interviewees expressed this in the following ways:

> You need to challenge these pathological beliefs because they are hooked up in their despair. (Int. 4).

Once the client has gone through and experienced what she is defending against, then she can move on. (Int. 2).

The client will grow as a result of going through the painful process of resolving their bereavement. (Int. 6).

Facilitating the release of painful emotion

As indicated in table A.7, this sub-core variable has seven broad categories of interventions and processes. The first category 'Facilitating the release of painful emotion' is concerned with the basic psychosocial process of the counsellor facilitating the release of painful emotion and, as a result of this emotional discharge, the client is able to consider his/her future in a more hopeful way. As stated in the introduction to this chapter, it may seem contradictory to suggest that enabling and encouraging someone to access their pain is hope inspiring. In order to consider this contradiction it is necessary and valuable to examine this process in more detail.

Perhaps some of the contradiction arises as a result of the current limited understanding of the dynamics of catharsis and hope inspiration. There is a fundamental difference between causing a person pain and helping a person to access pain that already exists. If any counsellor purposefully sets out to cause a client pain, then it is difficult to see how hope inspiration could occur from this. However, the counsellors in this study described no such activity; similarly such activity does not constitute part of the findings described in this book.

The counsellors, and subsequently the theory grounded in the data provided suggests that they facilitate a cathartic release. Which means to ease or expedite the release of painful and/or harmful emotions already present in the clients. According to the data obtained from both the counsellors and ex-clients, the presence of such painful feelings within the clients can hold them in a position of relative hopelessness. This hopelessness can fix them in the past; dwelling on what was; their pain is a constant reminder of what used to be; of what they have lost; that their hopes were dashed. Furthermore, data supplied by the ex-clients illustrated that it can be difficult for some clients to conceptualize any future where this pain is no longer their constant companion. Thus, any thoughts about the future, and these are likely to be limited, will centre on the perpetuation of their current state of emotional pain and on their hopelessness.

For the counsellors to facilitate the release of this painful emotion removes the 'emotional lodestone' that holds the clients in this fixed position of hopelessness. It brings relief, lightness to the clients' spirit. It enables to clients to begin to visualize a future that is pain free, that is less burdened with a sense of overwhelming loss; a future that is hopeful. The interviewees expressed this in the following ways:

> Some clients need to experience and release the maximum amount of their pain without being so distraught that they can't function, and it's about setting up the frame and the environment that enables them to do that. (Int. 8).

> She realized she could go through her crying, anger and emotional release and come out of the other side. (Int. 1).

> It could be that the way clients work with you gives them permission to cope with more pain than they would have done otherwise. (Int. 8).

> I encouraged her to experiment in not keeping the lid on her feelings. (Int. 4).

The ex-clients provided additional evidence of the hope inspiring value of releasing painful emotions. Their comments echoed and supported those of the counsellors. The ex-clients described this in the following ways:

> If you can share your pain with someone, have it acknowledged that someone has heard you, this is hugely valuable and hugely hope inspiring. (Int. 9).

> After I had discharged all that anger I felt so much lighter. Your head feels clearer. (Int. 11).

> I offloaded a lot of anger and I felt less burdened after that. (Int. 9).

> Letting my anger out in therapy was a key issue for me. (Int. 11).

> After I had discharged my pain, I felt sad but relieved. (Int. 9).

Supplying the opportunity for reflection

The second category 'Supplying the opportunity for reflection' is concerned with the basic psychosocial process of: the counsellor utilizing interventions to create or provide the opportunity for the clients to reflect. This category appears to have at least two properties, one that is concerned with the clients reflecting on their loss, and a further property that is concerned with the counsellors reflecting back certain feelings that they sense or words that they hear.

On first consideration, the first property may appear inappropriate as a potential means of hope inspiration, since it could be argued that encouraging clients to reflect on their loss could leave them floundering in sadness and hopelessness. However, the data gathered in this study suggest that the counsellors have the faith that such reflection is not necessarily harmful: if as a result of the reflection the clients raise some negative constructs, or disabling beliefs, this provides the counsellor with an opportunity for gentle and subtle challenging of these 'false' assumptions and constructs. That is not to say that the counsellor engages in cognitive therapy and begins to use Socratic questioning in order to illustrate to the clients that their thinking is not based on sound or reasoned thinking. It is more a matter of reflecting back to the clients that what they are describing are constructs, and not necessarily the 'truth'. For example, some clients described how they held beliefs that parents should always protect their children and keep them safe from harm. Consequently, when a child died from cancer, the parents were left feeling extremely guilty that they had somehow failed to protect their child from cancer and blamed themselves for the loss. In this situation the counsellor was able to reflect that back to the clients that, no doubt, parents often believe they should protect their children. Hence there is a subtle message conveyed here that what the clients are basing their guilt on is a belief. Simultaneously, the clients are being ushered into reflecting on how real the belief is that they can protect their children from cancer.

This subtle and gentle reflection provides the opportunity for clients to consider some of their negative assumptions and challenge some of their restrictive beliefs. When clients can begin to internalize that many of their beliefs about past failures, present limitations and future restrictions are based on unrealistic constructs and inaccurate self-perceptions, and are perpetuated by their current state of hopelessness, then they begin to challenge these perceptions and constructs for themselves. Clients begin to deconstruct some of their hopelessness and begin to construct a more hopeful future. The interviewees expressed this property of reflection and its hope inspiration potential in the following ways:

> There are hope inspiring ways of challenging clients' restrictive or disabling constructs. (Int. 7).

> What I do to challenge restrictive constructs is reflect back everything, no matter how minimal it sounds. (Int. 7).

> I may challenge some of the clients' expectations (the unrealistic ones), for example, that they expect to get their issues sorted out very quickly. (Int. 8).

> I will challenge some of their learned, restrictive responses to loss, but not in a very direct way. (Int. 7).

> I use statements that show up the person's restrictive constructs as exactly that, a construct, rather than being absolutely true. (Int. 7).

The ex-clients alluded to the use of gentle and subtle reflection by the therapist as a means of hope inspiration. Clients described how as a result of the reflection they received they realized that they needed to let go of some constructs and assumptions. It may be important to note that the ex-clients did not perceive this reflection and subsequent gentle challenge as forceful or damaging. However, what was felt to be important was, having offered the gentle challenge (e.g. challenging a particular defence mechanism), if the client chose not to address that issue at that particular time, the counsellors left well alone. They recognized that sometimes such defences can be healthy and that there would be further opportunities to address the defence mechanisms at a later point in the therapy. The ex-clients described this in the following ways:

> I had to acknowledge that my guilt was based on assumptions, and we challenged these. I am not superhuman. I had to acknowledge my own humanness. (Int. 10).

> My therapist gave me the words 'I wish' rather than 'I should have' (Int. 10).

> At times, the best thing for me was for the therapist to leave my defences well alone. (Int. 11).

The second property is concerned with the counsellors reflecting back certain feelings that they sense or words that they hear. As stated previously, the counsellors described how many clients had the need to release their repressed painful emotions, yet could be reluctant to do this and consequently, erected defence mechanisms. Despite these defences, it was common for the clients' feelings to permeate into the therapy. Due to the clients' defence mechanisms, this would not necessarily involve an overt expression of these feelings; however, the counsellors' sensitivity and empathy enabled them to get a 'felt sense' of the clients' feelings. It was of particular importance and value that the counsellors were aware of their own feelings. Feelings that the counsellors experienced for themselves during the therapy (e.g. feelings of sadness) were often an indication of feelings in the client during the therapy. As a result the counsellors were able to use whatever was 'going on' for them as a potential indication of what might be 'going on' for the client. Thus the counsellors would reflect the feelings they were experiencing. If this resonated with the clients; if the counsellors were sensing accurately some of what the clients were feeling, then this enabled the clients to be more open about their feelings and consequently enabled a catharsis of their repressed pain.

The interviewees expressed this second property of reflection and its hope inspiration potential in the following ways:

> If I felt the client had the need to release their pain, I would raise this with the client. I would reflect back my experience of them, how I experience their feelings, and ask them is that what is going on for you? (Int. 8).

> The counsellor tries to pick up on certain cues or intuitive 'felt senses' and these may prompt the counsellor to offer the client the opportunity to access and express their pain. (Int. 6).

> I pick up verbally and non-verbally the sorts of things that are issues for the clients. It is as much about what is not being said as what is being said. (Int. 8).

> If I can pick up, using advanced empathy, that the client has painful and unexpressed emotion, I may reflect back that it is ok for these emotions to be there. (Int. 6).

My skill of intuition plays a part. It is like, 'What have I tuned into?' and you get that confirmed one way or another by what the person says back to you. (Int. 8).

The ex-clients also alluded to this reflection of feelings sensed or perceived by the counsellors. At times the therapist's sense of the client's emotional state, and subsequent response to this perception, was precisely what the client needed at that moment in time. The ex-clients described how as a result of the reflection they received:

There were times when the therapist would pick up on my emotions, even though I hadn't expressed them overtly. (Int. 9).

My therapist reflected back the feelings he picked up from me. (Int. 11).

In response to long periods of silence and withdrawal he would remind me of his presence. He would not let me sit for over an hour in complete silence and despair. (Int. 11).

Providing unconditional and continual support

The third category, 'Providing unconditional and continual support' indicates that hope appears to be inspired as a result of the support the counsellors provide. This support appears to be manifest in three forms. The first form is the emotional/spiritual support; this has already been alluded to in the 'Forging the connection and relationship' sub-core variable (Chapter 4). The second form is the support provided by constructing a peaceful, non-threatening, and relaxing physical environment. The third form is in the help the counsellor provides to the client in identifying all different sources of support available to the client.

This emotional and spiritual support was bound up with the unconditional acceptance of the clients and whatever they say. However they feel, whatever emotions they express, this support would still be present. The data provided by the interviewees appears to indicate that this support helps the clients take risks. It provides an environment where they can expose their 'dark side' without the fear of rejection, further alienation or exacerbation of their loss and deepening of their sense of hopelessness. The data appeared to point out how emancipatory, liberating and hopeful it would feel to have the shackles of hopelessness and repression finally freed by the permissive and supportive environment generated by the counsellor.

The data gathered in this study indicate that perhaps hope flourishes and grows in a supportive environment. The literature review of this study indicated that hope looks to external help. One of the ways in which hope can be inspired in clients is the creation of a supportive environment by the counsellor. When one considers that hopelessness abounds in a destructive/disabling environment, the inverse becomes more evident: that hope abounds in a supportive environment. Hence increased support within the counselling environment can be equated with increased hope in the client.

While support has been identified within this sub-core variable, it would be inaccurate to limit the application and mobilization of support to only one component of this theory. Elements of support were present and evident in each category. Indeed, without a supportive underpinning, the value of the interventions indicated in this theory would be diminished, if not completely undermined. However, the use of support as a means to inspire hope also belongs as a separate category within this sub-core variable, as it was highlighted as a specific and separate process. This hope inspiring potential as a result of the supportive environment was expressed by the interviewees in the following ways:

> I recognize and acknowledge the clients' effort, the clients' difficulty; that it is painful to talk about such things. (Int. 8).

> Part of inspiring hope appears to involve identifying all the different types of support that the client has in their lives. (Int. 7).

> You can also provide support, and help the client to talk by considering the environment. (Int. 8).

> People want to be given permission to experience these feelings that they often feel embarrassed about. (Int. 8).

The ex-clients described the inspiration of hope through supporting the client. These people spoke of how supportive the counselling relationship and environment felt. They described how support was operationalized at various levels, and that feeling supported helped make the ex-clients feel more hopeful. The value of feeling supported as a means of helping the client feel more hopeful was described by the ex-clients in the following ways:

> I was supported by the counsellor in that I didn't have to justify my comments or make excuses for them, it was just accepted and that's the most important thing I can recall. (Int. 9).

> I felt support all the way through from the counsellor. (Int. 10).

> I thought and felt like I had a therapist who was very much on my side and supportive. (Int. 11).

> He would support me in 'getting on with it' and help me explore. (Int. 10).

> The therapist was aware that, 'Where is hope for that person?' when they have reached that position of silent withdrawal? (therefore offered support). (Int. 11).

> Even now, I can't ask for what I need, so she will intervene and do what she needs to do (which in this instance is come over and hold me while I cry). (Int. 12).

Freeing the client to talk about the deceased

This category indicates that hope appears to be inspired as a result of the clients feeling free and able to talk about the deceased in whatever ways are needed. The category contains at least two properties, one that is concerned with the particular hope inspiring value in being able to say negative things about the deceased, and a second that is concerned with clients being able to express such negative thoughts and feelings without driving the counsellor away. Part of this process appeared to be bound up with the dynamic of transference. The data gathered in this study indicates that this dynamic of transference allows and enables the clients to get angry, and say what they need to say, to the deceased. However, the way these thoughts and feelings are expressed makes it sound like it is the counsellor that the clients are angry with. Consequently, the negative thoughts and feelings that the clients have towards the deceased are then directed at the counsellor. This process may not sound particularly hope inspiring on first consideration. However, the hope inspiration appears to have two processes. First, for the clients to feel that they have the freedom to be able to do this, to know that it is ok, normal, common and indeed healthy offers the reassurance and thus hope that they are not 'bad people'. For the clients to come to understand that they can have and express such feelings without this being an indication of them being hopeless, allows them to feel more hopeful about themselves as people.

The second property indicates that clients are able to express such negative thoughts and feelings without driving the counsellor away, it conveys a message that the client is able to express these feelings and that this will not result in a further loss. The interviewees expressed this hope inspiration potential as a result of being able to express any negative thoughts or feelings about the deceased in the following ways:

> It sometimes helped the client, and they gained hope, from being able to talk openly about the negative aspects of the deceased. (Int. 3).

> If someone is angry with the deceased, I would encourage them to verbalize that. (Int. 6).

> Perhaps the vehicle of transference allows the client to tolerate more pain than perhaps they could otherwise be able to stand. (Int. 8).

The ex-clients also alluded to the inspiration of hope as a result of the clients feeling free and able to talk about the deceased in whatever ways are needed. Ex-clients spoke of the hope inspiring value in being able to say negative things about the deceased without feeling judged. They experienced a permissive environment where the expression of such thoughts and feelings did not exacerbate their perception of hopelessness. One ex-client described how, prior to entering into bereavement counselling, she was reluctant to say exactly what she felt: on the few occasions she had done this, she felt guilty afterwards and the guilt added to her sense of hopelessness. Consequently, when she then encountered the environment in the counselling, where there was an absence of guilt, blame or judgement, she learned to internalize this acceptance of her own feelings and realized that having such feelings was not uncommon. Furthermore, expressing such feelings brought her a sense of relief, made her feel as if a weight had been lifted from her shoulders and consequently helped her achieve a more hopeful perception. The ex-clients who stated this captured the value of feeling free and able to talk about the deceased in whatever ways are needed:

> Even though she was dead, it felt good to say things that I needed to say and not have someone become hysterical or scream or shout. (Int. 9).

> People are often unsure or don't feel that it is allowed to feel relieved that someone has died, or that they are glad that someone is dead. (Int. 9).

> I felt like I had landed in a place where I was allowed to have the good and the bad feelings about the person who had died. (Int. 9).

Employing therapeutic touch

This category indicates that hope appears to be inspired as a result of the therapist's use of therapeutic touch. It should be noted that this was only utilized at certain times during the therapy and as a result appeared to have had a particular powerful hope inspiring effect. Inversely, if used inappropriately, it could be disabling. The data gathered in this study indicate that perhaps this considered use of touch was at times the only way to connect with certain individuals. Additionally, for some people there appears to be great comfort and hope in the close physical presence of another human being. This physical presence may well include holding the client's hand, placing an arm around the client's shoulders or some other subtle such gesture. The interviewees described each of these physical interventions as a non-verbal method of communicating that someone cares.

While acknowledging the potential hope inspiring value of such interventions, counsellors were also mindful of the potential harm or disabling effect that clumsy or poorly timed physical therapeutic touch could have. Consequently, at these times, it was more hope inspiring for the counsellors not to touch the clients. This absence of touch did not equate with an absence of the counsellor's presence. Even though at these times no touch occurred, the counsellors would still be very much 'with' the client. Perhaps being silent, allowing the client the time and/or providing an environment where the client could processes his/her thoughts/feelings or express emotion as he/she needed to at that moment. This hope inspiration potential as a result of skillful and timely physical touch, and the comfort this brings was expressed by the interviewees in the following ways:

> When the client is totally withdrawn from me, the only thing that can get through to her is touch. (Int. 5).

> At the end of the session, when it is more informal, then I may put my hand on their shoulder. (Int. 1).

> What I tend to do is hold her hand. (Int. 5).

The ex-clients alluded to the appropriate and timely use of touch, and knowing when not to touch, as a means of hope inspiration. Ex-clients described the 'connectedness'; the sense of a strong and secure bond or relationship between themselves and the counsellors that was communicated by the use of touch. Furthermore, they alluded to how at times the last thing they wanted was to be 'overpowered' by too much inappropriate touch. The 'connectedness' was accompanied by a sense of safety and provided the ex-clients with something to 'hold onto'. One ex-client explained how as a result of feeling she had this 'anchor' to hold onto she was more prepared to experience the really powerful and painful emotions, and how consequently, the release of this intense pain gave her hope. The ex-clients described this in the following ways:

> I know there is a strong feeling of connectedness and security that can be conveyed by holding someone. I know this from my own children. (Int. 10)

> He was prepared to be physically close at times and this helped release the emotion. (Int. 10).

> The physical contact helps me to go to the places that are really scary, places that might be too scary to go to by myself. (Int. 10).

> At times my therapist used touch. An arm around my shoulder on the way out, something like that. (Int. 11).

> At times he was prepared to just hold me physically and be close. Or at times, not to hold me. (Int. 11).

I'm more likely to be 'huggy' if I'm happy. So somebody giving me a hug would interrupt what was going on for me. (Int. 9).

The lack of touch wasn't a problem for me as it gave me space within the therapy to work it out myself. (Int. 9).

Purposefully utilizing silence

This category indicates that hope appears to be inspired as a result of the therapist's purposeful use of silence. This was not an awkward silence that arose as a result of the counsellor feeling lost or incapable of responding to the clients. The purposeful use of silence means that the counsellor does not clutter the therapy with platitudes, unnecessary words, or attempts to 'fill' the quiet moments. The data gathered in this study indicate that this category appears to have two properties. First, the counsellors were mindful that such silence allows the clients to reflect, to be in touch with their thoughts/feelings, and enables the clients to discharge their painful emotions, for example, crying. Second, the purposeful silence and stillness allows the clients to get in touch with the hope that they do have. The interviewees described the hope inspiration potential as a result of the therapist's purposeful use of silence in the following ways:

Sometimes, perhaps the stillness can help the person get in touch with the little hope they have. (Int. 8).

If a client is in full flow, I say very little and attend to them. (Int. 6).

The purposeful use of silence allows people to track into their emotional self at a deeper level potentially, more so than if one communicated with them verbally. (Int. 8).

Stillness, for me, in bereavement is helping someone reach somewhere – a still centre. (Int. 6).

The ex-clients also described the therapist's use of silence and the effects that this silence and stillness had on them. The silence and stillness communicated a sense of permissiveness, a sense of freedom, a sense of 'connectedness'. Ex-clients spoke of how such silence communicated the counsellor's willingness to hear whatever the ex-client had to say. Such freedom and focused attention was in stark contrast to many of the ex-client's other relationships. What may be important to note is that during these still or silent times the ex-clients remained aware that the counsellor was still 'with them' and 'there for them'. They still encountered the counsellor's presence, the counsellor's demeanor and within that, implicitly, the counsellor's hopefulness. The ex-clients described this in the following ways:

> The counsellor used a lot of stillness and quietness in the therapy, and this enabled me to think about something I might have just said, or it gave me the space to cry. (Int. 9).

> The stillness was liberating, like being given a blank canvass. (Int. 11).

> When my therapist was still, it felt like, 'Anything goes. I can bring up and talk about anything I want to today.' (Int. 11).

> I never experienced those still moments as withdrawal by him. (Int. 11).

> At times I got a sense that my therapist was being very present, accepting and available whilst he was still. (Int. 11).

Avoiding colluding with the client's denial and/or hopelessness

This category indicates that hope appears to be inspired by another implicit message communicated by the therapist. Since the counsellors purposefully avoid colluding with the client's denial and hopelessness, they are conveying an implicit message that they consider that there is hope; that the future is not hopeless. The interviewees described this in the following ways:

> My work with her has been about confronting the reality of what's happened. (Int. 4).

> I will not collude to the extent that I will confirm the client's denial and say 'You are right, he is on holiday'. (Int. 7).

The essence of this category is captured by the ex-client's statement:

> At times I avoided issues, and she will pick up on it and say from her perspective that it feels like there could be a danger of her colluding with my avoidance. So she will acknowledge my denial, raise it into awareness but then won't push. (Int. 12).

6

Experiencing a Healthy [Good] Ending

In this chapter, I provide a detailed description of the processes and interventions that the bereavement counsellor can use to inspire hope in the sub-core variable 'experiencing a healthy [good] ending. This phase of the bereavement counselling encounter is concerned with the basic psychosocial processes of the client gaining hope from 'progressing through' and simultaneously experiencing a good and healthy ending. For clients to encounter such an experience illustrates to them that their current unhealthy, 'bad' ending can become a healthy, 'good' ending; that their current relatively hopeless position can become a hopeful one. Through having this experience, clients can realize that the outcome of bereavement need not be hopelessness. The inspiration of hope within this sub-core variable is bound up with the growth of self awareness in the clients. Furthermore, the sub-core variable is concerned with enabling the seed of hope within the client to grow and flourish.

If one accepts the axiom that the total absence of hope within a person is synonymous with a person's ultimate death, then each living person will have a seed or germ of hope that has the potential to be re-kindled. The client may well be unaware of such a seed, but the very fact that they keep on coming back for therapy is evidence of some hope in itself. The data gathered in this study indicates that clients describe the re-emergence of hope during their therapy. In particular they describe a more hopeful position, outlook and 'state of being' when the therapy is concluded. This sub-core variable also highlights how, perhaps, paradoxically this process of hope inspiration involves acknowledging the client's initial relative position of hopelessness. Then, by working with any restrictive, learned, early experiences of loss, by keying into the client's personal attributes and using them as a resource, by helping the client in achieving any particular tasks of grieving they may have, by reflecting on the positive and acknowledging the subtle growth in awareness as the therapy continues, by being aware of and looking for subtle changes in orientation, and building upon them, the seed of hope is nurtured. This nurturing of the clients' seed of hope and the clients' more hopeful state of being after the conclusion of the therapy was expressed by the interviewees in the following ways:

> Since the client has had the experience of a very unhealthy ending, I think providing an ending that clients can have some control over, gives them some hope. (Int. 4).

> After the therapy I felt, 'Right, it's all tied up now, we can really move on.' (Int. 9).

> After the therapy there was a definite sense of moving on, I was more future orientated. (Int. 9).

> I felt more hopeful at the end of therapy than I did at the beginning. (Int. 9).

Realizing the potential for growth in bereavement

As indicated in table A.8, this sub-core variable has five broad categories of interventions and processes. The first category 'realising the potential for growth in bereavement' is concerned with developing the awareness that a person can experience bereavement and come through it and even grow. The data appear to demonstrate that even in (or after) a bereavement, there is still hope. That one can endure pain, survive it and look forward to the remainder of one's life. As the client and the counsellor work towards their own endings within the therapy, and as the counsellor models his/her own genuine and 'healthy' response to bereavement, the client begins to realize and internalize the awareness that loss does not necessarily result in a sense of hopelessness.

There appear to be two properties to this process. One property is concerned with the intrapersonal processes within the client. Throughout the therapy, the issues of ending mirror those issues in ending in the clients' bereavement. As a result, the clients are ushered into a process of experiential learning. They learn for themselves that loss does not have to result in hopelessness. They learn that an outcome of loss can be a hopeful position. The second property is concerned with the interpersonal processes. The clients are guided through this process of healthy grieving by the modeling that the counsellor undertakes. They witness the counsellor experiencing the loss and yet the counsellor is not destroyed by it; they do not finish with a sense of hopelessness. As with the intrapersonal process, a result of this modeling is an increased awareness in the clients that loss does not have to mean hopelessness. The essence of this process was summed up by one interviewee who stated:

> Modelling a healthy response in itself inspires hope, it really does, because people get into repeats and can thus do something different to what they were allowed to do before. (Int. 7).

The ex-clients also described the change in themselves as a result of receiving therapy. Not only did the ex-clients undergo a movement towards a more hopeful position, but crucially, they gained an awareness of this change and were able to internalize the reality that they had gained hope from the process of bereavement counselling. The ex-clients alluded to the mirroring that took place, the similarities between the experiences of ending in the therapy and in the ex-clients' lives. Ex-clients described how they were aware of the counsellor's own response to the loss as it was told. Not only were the counsellors not shocked by any disclosure or expression of emotion, but importantly, the ex-clients noticed that the counsellors were comfortable with expressing their own sadness. As a result of these intra- and interpersonal processes the ex-clients illustrated that they gained hope and felt more hopeful. Perhaps the clients had even grown from the experience of bereavement counselling and reaching a more hopeful position than they had previously attained. This was described by the ex-clients in the following ways:

> I would leave the therapy with a change in a spiritual sense. A very warm, positive feeling, the sense of optimism which wasn't there an hour before. (Int. 11).

> One of the most vital things that therapy offered me was that it was one of my first healthy clear experiences of ending. (Int. 11).

> There were parallels in the ending of the therapy and the ending with my loved one. But it was noticeable that I could prepare myself for the ending in the therapy and that is definitely better. (Int. 10).

> At the end of the therapy, I ended up at a higher point, a more hopeful point, than I had ever been before. (Int. 11).

Avoiding repeats

The category 'avoiding repeats' indicates that hope inspired by the client avoiding any repeats of their previous, learned, restrictive methods of reacting to bereavement. Bound up with this process is the client's previous experience of loss. The interviewees described how ex-clients experienced difficulties when dealing with their loss as a result of the restrictions imposed upon them by their significant others. Often such restrictions had been 'learned' during previous experiences of loss. For example, the interviewees stated:

> During her previous loss, the family had openly discouraged any grieving. So my client had to deal with all this learned stuff. (Int. 7).

> The client had never had the opportunity to express her true feelings about the loss. (Int. 8).

> It was only when she started to get angry about her previous loss, and not being able to grieve for her, this marked a turning point and she was better able to grieve for the current loss. (Int. 7).

Experiencing a healthy ending enables the client to 'throw off' these learned restrictions and respond to the loss in any way that they need to. The data appeared to suggest how hope inspiring it would be for clients to be able to finally begin to say all those things that they needed to say, to do all those things that they needed to do in response to the loss and finally carry out the actions which they have been denied as a result of the restrictions imposed upon them.

This category appears to have two properties of hope inspiration. The first is concerned with the lifting of the restrictions; in itself this may well be hope inspiring and then as a result of the absence of restrictions one can begin the process of ventilating feelings. The inspiration is particularly powerful where clients find themselves in a repeating pattern of dynamics. It is distinctly possible that people can get into 'cycles of bereavement'. If clients have any previous 'learning' regarding the suppression of any feelings of loss in an earlier bereavement, these clients bring with them into therapy an expectation that the counsellor will similarly repress such expression.

The second property is concerned with the 'learned' expectation and centres on the client's belief that if he/she shares any of his/her feelings, then the counsellor will abandon him/her. If their past experiences of loss have 'taught' the clients that if they express any of their feelings over the loss, then people will abandon them, then this expectation is likely to repeated within the therapy. Thus, the counsellor being tenacious, being committed to the client and to the process of the therapy, does much to counter many of those learned and restrictive responses to loss. So the counsellors described how they are genuine, open and transparent in their reaction to the client's loss, and there is no withdrawal on the part of the counsellor in response to what the client shares. This acceptance and commitment challenges any expectations founded in the client's previous experiences of loss.

This avoidance of repeating learned, restrictive responses to loss was pointed out by the ex-clients. One ex-client, who received therapy for two significant losses in his life, alluded to his learned responses. He explained that his reaction to his first loss was influenced by his early experiences of loss, where he had not been encouraged to engage in open expression of sadness. He needed to 'learn' to experience his grief in any way he wanted to as a result of encountering the accepting, supporting and permissive environment and attitude of his counsellor. Having experienced this healthier way of responding to his loss, he became more hopeful, he was better equipped to respond to his second significant loss in a way that he was more comfortable with. This was described by the ex-client in the following ways:

I dealt with the loss of my father much better (than my previous loss) having worked through that previous loss in therapy. (Int. 11).

Much of my therapy at that time has been influenced by the ending of my previous relationship. (Int. 11).

Accomplishing any tasks of bereavement

The next category, 'Accomplishing any tasks of bereavement' indicates that hope is inspired by clients accomplishing any individual tasks of bereavement. The interviewees described that some people feel they need to carry out certain tasks of bereavement. It is important to note that such tasks were not imposed onto the client from the counsellor's agenda. The clients are either already aware of this need in themselves or they became aware of such tasks as the therapy progressed. However, if the counsellor gained the sense that clients wished to carry out such tasks, then they were encouraged and supported to do so. This was described by the interviewees in the following ways:

Clients often have unfinished business around the relationship (with the deceased) and these can be addressed in the therapy. (Int. 8).

Because I am now much more experienced in bereavement counselling, I do not suggest that people carry out certain tasks. But I would support someone in carrying out the tasks they identify. (Int. 7).

Viewing the photographs of the dead child may have been one of the tasks of her bereavement. (Int. 7).

As a consequence of carrying these tasks out, the ex-clients felt a sense of accomplishment, felt they were moving towards closure, felt they were starting to relocate the deceased in an emotional sense, and they became more hopeful. As indicated in the earlier portion of this book, for many groups of people hope is concerned with an expectation of some future event. The data obtained in this study appear to suggest that when such expectations are met, when such tasks are completed, then hope is gained. In the same way that hopelessness can become a self perpetuating phenomenon (i.e. it is not self limiting, hopelessness begets hopelessness) so too can hope. Achieved or actualized hopes beget further hope. By helping the client to identify and achieve any tasks of bereavement he/she may have, the counsellor is nurturing and inspiring hope.

The ex-clients also referred to the value and difficulty in accomplishing any tasks of bereavement that they had. Not only did ex-clients become aware of these tasks or that they had unfinished business, but having become aware of these issues, they were then able to be supported in accomplishing them. While acknowledging that carrying out any such tasks could be a difficult process, having accomplished such tasks, the ex-clients did experience a greater sense of hope and hopefulness. This appeared to be as a result of attaining a difficult goal (i.e. accomplishing the task) and also that attaining these goals symbolized progression and movement through their process of grieving. This was described by the ex-clients in the following ways:

> We acknowledged in therapy that dealing with certain tasks of bereavement is hard. (Int. 10).

> I became aware of the need to carry out certain tasks as a result of the therapy, at least in part anyway. (Int. 9).

> The counsellor encouraged me to carry out the bereavement tasks that I brought up, such as reading some of her poetry, cleaning out her house. (Int. 9).

Ensuring clients retain control

The next category 'Ensuring clients retain control' indicates how hope is inspired in clients, by the counsellor ensuring the clients retain control. As a result of feeling that they have control, the clients feel less powerless, less 'done unto', less manipulated by events. It is an experience that is likely to be contrary to the experience of their loss, where the clients felt entirely out of control and helpless. The data obtained in this study appear to indicate that as a result of feeling that they have an element of control, the clients feel more hopeful. This control was evident in a number of realms.

The first is the realm of the expression of emotions. Although the counsellors may have felt that the clients would benefit from expressing any repressed negative or painful emotion, the clients retained control over how and when they expressed these feelings. Even though counsellors may use a confrontative intervention to raise the matter of repressed material into the client's consciousness, the choice concerning whether or not to express this material remained with the client.

The second realm is that of the nature of the clients' response to the loss. As stated previously, in contrast to some previous 'learned' responses to loss, the clients have control (and freedom) over how they respond to the bereavement. Many clients had been actively discouraged from any open expression of feelings concerning the loss of their loved one. Consequently, counsellors were careful to create and provide a permissive atmosphere and environment, contrary to the clients' previous early experiences, an atmosphere where the clients had control, where the clients decided how they would respond to the bereavement.

The third realm is that of the clients' particular tasks of bereavement. As stated previously, where the clients feel they have specific tasks of bereavement, the counsellors would encourage and support the clients to carry out these tasks. However, the clients retain the control and subsequently decided how and when they carry out any tasks of bereavement. The hope inspiring potential of ensuring the clients retain as much control as possible was described by the interviewees in the following ways:

> As I work in a person centered way, my starting point is always going to be wherever the client is. (Int. 7).

> The counsellor followed the client's lead. (Int. 3).

> There were times that I got a sense that something would be worth addressing but the client could/would not share that at that time. (Int. 5).

> I would point out that there is avoidance going on, but it is up to the client to decide whether or not she addresses these issues then and there. (Int. 5).

The fourth realm is concerned with control over the timing and nature of the ending of the therapy, and it should be noted that the ex-clients and counsellors indicated that this realm may have greater importance than the previous three realms. Clients had and exercised significant control over the timing and nature of the ending of the therapy. The control over the ending in the therapy is considered early in the process, indeed, as soon as the issue of ending the therapy is introduced. Counsellors described that sometimes there would be a re-negotiation of the date for ending, with clients becoming anxious as the ending approaches. This negotiated ending is also dissimilar from the clients' experience of bereavement where it is unlikely that they negotiated an ending with the deceased. The ex-clients spoke of how they retained an element of control over the ending in the therapy and how this was a positive experience for them. The ex-clients were able to juxtapose their experiences of ending in the therapy with their experiences of ending in their loss. This sense of having a degree of control was regarded as important otherwise the ending would serve as a repeat of their previous loss. The data in this study appeared to indicate that such repeats would serve only to add to the clients' perception and experience of hopelessness. For them to experience an ending that they did have some control over had the opposite effect and helped the ex-clients to experience more hope and hopefulness. This was described by the ex-clients in the following ways:

> The therapy ended slowly over time. I think I was weaned off him. (Int. 10).

> In order to work towards an ending we planned a date, we made sure there were enough sessions, we negotiated the ending really. (Int. 9).

> The ending in the therapy was very different to the other ending (i.e. loss) in that it wasn't imposed upon me. There was no sense of betrayal. (Int. 11).

> We did work towards an ending in the therapy, it was something I needed to do. (Int. 9).

> The ending was negotiated. I had some control over it. (Int. 11).

> Having a sense of control over the ending, time to prepare is important, essential. (Int. 10).

Increasing the client's self-awareness

The next category 'increasing the client's self-awareness' indicates how the inspiration of hope appears to be bound up with the growth of self-awareness within the client. The data in this study suggests that this category has at least four properties. The first property focuses on the process where, as clients become more self-aware, they realize that they do have choices and options. They begin to internalize that they do not have to accept and endure their hopelessness; that they can do something about it; that they can have a hopeful future.

The second property focuses on the process where the growth of self-awareness in the clients enables them to acknowledge their current 'emotional position' and importantly, to become aware that they do not want to be there, that they want to be in a different place. This very act of visualizing or conceptualizing themselves being in a different emotional place is an indication of a more hopeful state of being. Each small step that the clients take towards this more hopeful position then adds to their hope. This second property warrants further explanation. As indicated previously, hopelessness begets hopelessness; it is not a self-limiting process. It appears that movement towards being more hopeful begets a more hopeful state of being. The act of visualising a more hopeful emotional place thus inspires hope. This very process of hoping demonstrates to the clients that they can be more hopeful.

The third property focuses on the process where the growth of self-awareness in the clients also enables them to realize that they do not have to comply with the hopelessness-inducing restrictions that some significant people impose upon them. The awareness brings with it the appreciation that the clients have the right and the freedom to react to and grieve in response to their loss in any way that they want. As a result of the removal of these impositions and restrictions, the clients are therefore more able to express any repressed pain or feelings.

The fourth property focuses on the process where, as a result of growth in their self-awareness, clients are more able to identify the positive steps they have taken since the bereavement and the positive steps they have taken within the therapy. Sometimes the clients are not aware that they have made any progress during the therapy. Furthermore, clients sometimes have difficulty accepting that they have made progress. The clients become so accustomed to having little sense of hope or hopefulness and are so acclimatized to expressing life in hopeless terms, that they have a problem conceptualizing themselves in any way that indicates a more hopeful outlook. Thus, as a consequence of growth in their self-awareness, clients can begin to recognize and accept that they have moved on, have even grown; that they have started to deal with issues during the therapy. When clients can reflect on the progress they have made during the therapy, they gain a sense of hope and become more hopeful. The potential for hope inspiration as a result of the growth of awareness was expressed by the ex-clients in the following ways:

> There was a gradual growing of awareness that the spells of having more of a sense of 'well-being' started to get longer. (Int. 10).

> There was a change in the way I viewed the future. I can say that looking back now. (Int. 10).

> At the end of the therapy I felt like I was in a different place, a higher point, a different sense of myself. (Int. 11).

> It's like knowing that whilst I have been to a horrible place before, I have some way of being, some inner strength and a support system that enables me to know that if I drop back into something despairing again, then I can cope. (Int. 10).

> After the session on my way home, I would be aware that things are changing, like a seed had been planted and was beginning to grow on my way home. (Int. 11).

> I gained an awareness of these differences as time (and the therapy) went on. Even subtle changes of how I felt. (Int. 10).

> I was able to gradually get a sense of the differences in me; differences in terms of my perspectives. (Int. 10).

> This growing awareness made me aware of the fluidity rather than the 'stuckness'. (Int. 10).

> In the end I realized it was time for me to move on; to realize that there are positive things that can come from this. (Int. 10).

Similarly, the interviewees alluded to the hope inspiring value of the growth of awareness in the clients. They expressed this in the following ways:

> The clients' hope comes, in part, from realising where they are at the moment; acknowledging that they don't want to be there, and from wanting to be in a different place. (Int. 8).

By enabling people to explore the more emotional aspects of themselves, they start to consider their own hope they have, that they will actually get over this. (Int. 8).

When clients start to internalize the messages of acceptance, they begin to accept their grief and pain and get angry at those people who try to restrict them from being sad. (Int. 7).

PART THREE

Implications for Research, Policy and Practice

7

Fit for Purpose?

Implications for Education and Training

In Chapter 1, I indicated how attempts have been made to define and understand hope within healthcare and associated literature from the 1960s. The focus of the writing on hope during the 1960s appeared to be concerned with philosophical, theological and theoretical debate around the nature of hope. By the 1980s the focus had shifted towards defining hope in specific groups and to determining its influence in specific nursing situations. During the 1990s the limited number of studies have been concerned with determining how to inspire hope in specific client groups.

However, within this limited literature there is a common finding: that of the alleged centrality and distinct therapeutic potential of hope – one echoed by the findings in this book. Given this alleged value and potential, one could be forgiven for expecting to encounter far more research and a far greater number of discussion papers on hope. Yet, as previously indicated, there is a distinct dearth of such papers. This disparity begs the question: if hope is so important, central and potentially valuable, then why isn't there more written about it and why isn't there more research evidence available?

In response to this question, the findings from my study indicate how implicit, subtle and unobtrusive the inspiration of hope appears to be. Similarly, clients were aware of hope only to the degree that they did not possess much of it. One seems to become more aware of hope when one has need of it. Whilst the counsellors alluded to the importance of hope, they similarly declared that, in order for such hope to be therapeutic, it needed to remain implicit. It is perhaps not surprising then that the basic, yet important, social process of hope inspiration has had minimum attention paid to it previously in the relevant empirical literature. In the same way that Lynch (1965) posited that one does not draw breath hoping consciously that it will sustain life, counsellors do not appear to engage in bereavement counselling with the explicit pretext that they are there to inspire hope. The hope inspiration is bound up with their practice, embedded within the counsellor's clinical expertise.

If this argument is cogent, then it further illustrates why there is only limited literature on the nature of hope inspiration. Counselling (and nursing) research have a history of being influenced by the medical profession (see for example the arguments of Pearson 1992). Consequently, the philosophical and epistemological beliefs and methodological nuances of the bio-medical model have been adopted by some nurse/counselling researchers. Thus, positivistic philosophies, quantitative methods, and the hegemony of randomized control trial designs can be seen throughout many research reports (Cutcliffe 1998), including many of those that focused on the concept of hope (see Kylma and Vehvilainen-Julkunen 1997). Few studies (or researchers) have been concerned with obtaining 'know-how' knowledge, the knowledge embedded in clinical practice (Benner 1984). Indeed, Pearson (1992) points out

> much of our scholarly theorizing is only distantly related to the real world of practicing nurses, especially when it utilizes the most rigorous methods of positivism, the mechanistic application of problem solving, or attempts to reduce and categorize the phenomena encountered in nursing. (p.222)

Consequently, the absence of evidence within the relevant empirical literature highlighting the alleged importance, centrality and potentially therapeutic value of hope can be attributed, in part, to the prevailing preoccupation of some within counselling research (and nursing research) with the deductive paradigm.

Hope inspiration and bereavement counselling training

Whether current bereavement counselling training prepares therapists adequately in the theory and practice of hope inspiration is a difficult question to answer. First, it is hard to determine how much attention is currently paid to matters of hope inspiration within formal bereavement counselling training (or generic counselling training, for that matter). Whilst survey research has been carried out almost every year to determine the content of formal preparation for community psychiatric nurses (e.g. see Bowers' research, or Hannigan's research), there is no such study evident in the literature that examines the extent of attention paid to hope inspiration within formal bereavement counselling training. However, informal conversations and canvassing of many counsellors and therapists tentatively suggest that little (if any) attention is paid to hope inspiration in training, and this is reflected in the relevant bereavement counselling literature. However, such 'findings' need to be treated with caution, making it difficult to say, with any conviction, that as a result of this absence of explicit attention to hope current training is either adequate or inadequate.

It is also fair to say that formal counselling training is by no means the only place where professional development and education of counsellors occur. The counsellors in the study were aware that hope was an issue; thus one might speculate that bereavement counsellors are far from ignorant of issues pertaining to hope inspiration, certainly given the rich data provided by the counsellors. This in turn indicates something of the unique value of grounded theory studies, in which they make explicit and overt the theory that is implicit and which underpins practice.

It appears that bereavement counsellors (at least the bereavement counsellors in this study) do have some knowledge and awareness of issues and concerns of hope inspiration, despite the apparent absence of these within formal counselling training. Whilst it is heartening just to see some evidence of such awareness, my findings strongly indicate that hope plays an important and valuable role in bereavement counselling. In my view, there is, therefore, a strong case for revisiting course curricula and including the theory of the inspiration of hope, in formal bereavement counselling training and (arguably) generic counselling training. This would mean that future generations of counsellors and therapists would have a strong evidence base to their work with clients who are experiencing a complicated grief reaction. They will then be able to develop and modify this theory as new demands, new situations and new challenges arise.

Mental health practitioner training

It is unlikely that current mental health nurse training, with its emphasis on neurobiology and masculine approaches to care, adequately prepares aspirant mental health nurses for the methods of practice or ways of working with people identified in this study. (For the purposes of discussion, I am adopting Barker's (1999) conceptualisation of masculine approaches to care, i.e. care concerned with 'experts' external to the individual 'fixing' the recipient of care. Power resides with the practitioner and the system.)

Many of the methods for inspiring hope are 'invisible' or of 'low visibility' (Altschul 1997; Brown and Fowler 1979; Micheal 1994). It can be argued that, in order for practitioners to inspire hope, using these low-visibility methods requires a degree of faith: faith, belief and hope in the process, in the person and in themselves. Furthermore, it is evident that many of the methods of hope inspiration are not congruent with fixed, rigid, predictable approaches to care. As mentioned earlier, many experienced or expert P/MH nurses appear to feel comfortable with such uncertainty. However, according to Cutcliffe and Goward (2000), reaching a position where the mental health nurse is comfortable with diversity is not an easy process. Students as aspiring P/MH nurses often begin this process by seeking out premature consensus and a firm relationship between processes and outcomes. This search for consensus may be manifested in early attempts to locate themselves within an essentially humanistic, psychodynamic or behaviourist paradigm at the expense of others. Alternatively, the search for consensus may be pursued by attempts to 'hang' their theory and practice on tangible, overt interventions. For many aspirant mental health nurses there is a need to be seen to be doing; to feel that they are making a difference.

As indicated in Chapter 3, in addition to early requirements for a sense of certainty, there can be a corresponding reluctance in aspirant mental health nurses to encourage clients to express emotion. Too often mental health practitioners concern themselves with attempts to contain and fix, when what they should be doing is freeing the restraints on people. The counsellors in this study make reference to this need to allow people to fall apart in a supportive, rather than a restrictive environment – to throw off the 'shackles' of previous restrictive and disabling relationships in order that they might gain hope as a result of expressing their painful emotions.

It becomes clear, therefore, that there is a clear need for practitioners to be comfortable with the free expression of emotion.

However, it would be inappropriate to criticize mental health nurses for not exhibiting such behaviour when their training or preparation has not equipped them with such attitudes, knowledge or skills. It is unlikely that current mental health nurse training, with its emphasis on neurobiology and masculine approaches to care, adequately prepares aspirant mental health nurses for such methods of practice. Barker (1999a) makes reference to this shortfall suggesting:

> In the UK, nurses receive only limited preparation for psycho-therapeutic work, as part of their basic education. (p.174)

Hence, in order to maximize the potential for inspiring hope through the use of the theory of the inspiration of hope, there is a need to improve the preparation of mental health nursing students for psychotherapeutic work.

The desire to see the development of mental health nurse training include more training in psychotherapeutic approaches to care is not evidence of a fanciful, unrealistic or utopian attitude to mental health nurse preparation. This is not an unattainable goal: it is one advocated by many mental health nursing scholars, academics and educationalists. Barker (1999a) points out that:

> A growing body of literature suggests the possible diversity of psychotherapeutic roles and functions which might be fulfilled by nurses providing that they receive appropriate training and clinical supervision. (p.176)

The 1982 psychiatric nursing syllabus increasingly systematized the philosophy of learning from experience, emphasising group dynamics and psychodynamics (Ritter 1997). Parkes (1997) reasoned in favour of a psychiatric nursing education system that encourages reflective thinking and exploration of personal values as well as a focus on self-awareness. Consequently, it can be seen that the infrastructure and theoretical body of knowledge already exists (or has existed) for preparing mental health nurses to work in psychotherapeutic ways with clients. Accordingly, it would be an appropriate step to interweave the findings of my study into such mental health nurse preparation and to include an examination of the ways in which nurses can inspire hope as part of that preparation.

8

Implications for Research and Policy

Is there a genetic answer?

In the 'decade of the brain' should researchers be more concerned with identifying a 'hope gene' or a 'hopelessness gene' and less concerned with social processes of hope inspiration?

During the 1930s the prevailing orthodoxy regarded the mind as an extended function of the brain. Currently within the field of psychiatry and mental health care (including some schools of counselling and therapy) there is evidence that some have returned to such neo-Darwinian perspectives of the mind. Barker (1999a, p.143) pointed out that, in less than 50 years, the knowledge base of psychiatry has shifted from the assumption that the many variants of human personality are largely a function of the lived experience, to the assumption that the mind is largely a function of genetic influence. According to Lego (1999), further evidence of this emphasis can be seen in psychiatry's move towards neurobiology, prompted by enormous pressure from the pharmaceutical industry, which results in a view of the person in need of mental health care as the brain in need of chemical intervention.

Such beliefs concerning the nature of person, brain and mind invite the question: if the mind is merely a function of genetics, then what good or value is hope? Furthermore, what good is a study of this kind? What purpose does it serve? In response to these questions: if minds are biological entities, then there appears to be little value in examining spiritual, social and interpersonal processes. Instead, perhaps studies should focus on the search for, and subsequent isolation of, a 'hope gene' or 'hopelessness gene'.

However, such assumptions and attitudes are anathema to the views of the mind as a product of a person's lived experience and, more important, do not accord with the findings obtained in this study. The notion of human responses to individuals in need of mental health care is not new. Since the 1950s the work of Peplau (1988), Sullivan (1952) and Rogers (1952) amongst others has asserted the position that nurse therapists and mental health nurses think exclusively of patients as persons, focus on the whole person, and help people discover the meaning of their experiences.

Furthermore, the view of the person as merely a brain, and of the mind as little more than the product of genetic influence, are clearly at odds with the views of the very individuals who require and receive mental health care. In the largest study of users' appreciation of psychiatric services in the UK, Rogers, Pilgrim and Lacey (1993) found that a preferred model of practice involved personal contact and understanding, being listened to and responded to empathetically. These findings are frequently echoed in studies from around the world, where evidence affirms the essential features of mental health nursing (and therapy) and what users want from their mental health practitioners and therapists. For example, the studies of McIntyre, Farrell and David (1989), Beech and Norman (1995) and Rudman (1996) all indicate what users of mental health care found to be important aspects of their care. McIntyre, Ferrell and David (1989) carried out a survey of 99 in-patients in an inner London psychiatric hospital. Beech and Norman (1995) used a critical incident analysis technique in a field study to gather incidents of high- and low-quality care as perceived by 24 in-patients with mental health problems. Rudman (1996) used a grounded-theory method to elicit the views of 20 users of a pre-registration nursing curriculum. Each of these studies indicates that it is the presence of the quality of caring, the relationship established with the staff and the human connection that users value the most and want from their service.

Similarly, in a survey of users' views of their continuing care community service that had a response rate of 81 per cent, Cutcliffe *et al.* (1997) found that users appear to regard as important those nursing interventions that are concerned with providing emotional support. These findings are in keeping with the studies of Gordon, Alexander and Dietzan (1979), Elbeck and Fecteau (1990), and Beech and Norman (1995). Each of these studies report that users value interpersonal relationships with mental health nurses and therapists very highly and that this is often what leads to high user satisfaction. The most recent research findings emanating from the Mental Health Foundation report *Strategies for Living* (2000), again reiterated the centrality of accepting relationships and the value users place on such relationships. What users want from their therapists and mental health nurses is best summarized by the survivor Peter Campbell (1997), who asserted that psychiatric services can suffer from an excess of Yang, of attempts to contain and fix, when what users want is nurses to work alongside users – shifting the emphasis away from neurobiology, genetics and pharmacology and towards the interpersonal aspects, the human–human connection, and the search for meaning. All of which were identified in my study as being bound up with the inspiration of hope.

Inspiring hope: too time-consuming?

Any theory that is generated with the purpose of addressing issues arising in healthcare, ground-breaking or praiseworthy as it may be, cannot have its merit, applicability or worth determined in isolation. Theory pertaining to healthcare has to be considered within the wider context of healthcare policy, healthcare resources and economics. So, the application of the theory of hope inspiration within bereavement counselling may be inhibited by market forces, the pressures of economic restraints and current preoccupations with 'quick fixes'. How, then, could current policy initiatives, healthcare resources and economics within the National Health Service impact on the application of this theory?

The theory of hope inspiration within bereavement counselling suggests that some clients need time to form the connection and relationship; to gain the sense of trust; to begin to ventilate the painful emotion and to work towards an ending. This need for time was captured by ex-clients' statements:

> It was not a simple, linear flow from despair to hope. It was more a matter of a journey. Three steps forward, two steps back.

> Time was a factor in enabling me to go from a despairing position to a more hopeful one.

Perhaps within bereavement counselling time is of particular importance. As pointed out previously, in some cases part of the processes of hope inspiration and resolving a complicated bereavement may involve going back and re-investing in an intimate trusting relationship. For some, this learning to trust again, learning to be intimate again, is realized in the relationship forged between the client and counsellor. Unfortunately, due to the nature of their reaction to loss, some clients are resistant to such relationship formation for fear of losing someone else and adding to their loss and pain. Consequently, this learning to trust again, learning to be intimate again, can take time.

However, the current policy (e.g. within the NHS in the UK and NHS counselling services) is shifting the emphasis away from longer-term intensive approaches to counselling (e.g. humanistic/ person-centred and psychodynamic/psychoanalytical) towards brief solution therapy or cognitive-behavioural approaches. These approaches are associated with fewer client/counsellor sessions and are therefore cheaper (Barker 1999b; Lego 1998). Additional changes are evident in counselling practice where some healthcare providers have encouraged an increase in the use of group therapy in place of individual therapy. According to Lego (1999) the movement away from psychotherapy was, and is, economically driven. In addition, current healthcare initiatives proposed by the government can be seen to provide further evidence of the current accentuation of short-term intervention strategies or, to use a more colloquial expression, 'quick fixes'. For example, the introduction of telephone counselling, and telephone healthcare lines such as 'NHS Direct' in the UK, whilst no doubt laudable practices in their own right, and no doubt meeting the requirements of some people in need of mental health care, are also inextricably linked to cost cutting, reducing waiting lists, and constitute evidence of 'the quick fix'.

However, the findings in my study indicate that for people experiencing a complicated bereavement and consequently in need of hope, quick fixes may not be appropriate. That is not to suggest that every individual who requires bereavement will need 'long-drawn-out' therapy. What my research findings do appear to indicate, however, is that there is still a need for bereavement counselling for some, that is not quick-fix-orientated, particularly for some clients with complicated grief reactions. To deny such clients the opportunity for longer therapy is to deny them the chance of having hope inspired in them as a result of their therapy.

Credibility in a technocratic world

The findings in this book may perhaps have little credibility for some who operate in a world (and healthcare system) that is preoccupied with measurable outcomes and masculine approaches to care. Recently, the English National Board for Nurses, Midwives and Health Visitors (1997) reiterated that nurse training should produce practitioners who are fit for purpose, with the emphasis within nurse preparation being on the acquisition of appropriate skills. Similarly, the Sainsbury Centre document *Pulling Together: The Future Roles and Training of Mental Health Staff* (1997) describes what it sees as the core skills, knowledge and attitudes required in mental health services. It is important to note that the Sainsbury Centre's recommendations are not limited to nurses, but to the variety of disciplines involved in mental health care, including counsellors and therapists. The core skills are divided into four areas: management and administration; assessment; treatment and care management; and collaborative working. It may be worth noting that none of these four areas of core skill development makes any reference to the development of person-centred or humanistic qualities, despite its reference to the importance of attitudes. Furthermore, particular ways to inspire hope are similarly absent. Perhaps the only two core competencies that hint at the development of the appropriate qualities are those that refer to the acquisition of knowledge and skill in effective interpersonal communication, and in creating therapeutic co-operation and developing an alliance with the service user. It is evident, therefore, that current preparation of mental health practitioners (including counsellors) appears to have a clear emphasis on overt, tangible, highly visible skills acquisition.

Consequently, when considering how to inspire hope in bereavement counselling, there may be some demand to identify highly visible, tangible, skills-based interventions or even clearly identified critical-care pathways. This is in order to comply with current attitudes regarding adequate practitioner preparation. It can be argued that the findings from this research do not supply such overt skills-based approaches to hope inspiration. Therefore, it can be seen that for some, the findings of this study may lack credibility.

Nevertheless, this may not be the position adopted by all mental healthcare practitioners. The notion of the invisibility of some psychiatric/mental health nurse (and counselling) activity has been posited by several authors recently (see Altschul 1997; Cutcliffe 1998; Michael 1994). This is not a new perspective: over 20 years ago Brown and Fowler (1979) referred to the work of P/MH nurses as consisting of high- and low-visibility functions. More recently, Cutcliffe and Goward (2000) have argued that the presence of uncertainty does not appear to be a hindrance for mental health care practitioners. In a healthcare world characterized by ambiguity, where the outcomes and processes of mental health care are not wholly congruent with fixed, rigid and predictable views of the world, it may not be possible to provide high visibility, tangible, overt interventions. However, Cutcliffe and Goward (2000) reason that the absence of such clearly marked paths is not problematic for some mental health care practitioners. Indeed Dawson (1997) argues that many people in need of some form of mental health care may not benefit from rigid positivistic-based approaches to care: a position supported by Barker (1997) who suggests that skilled mental health practitioners are influenced by an unconscious perception of chaos as their guide to understanding the human condition and do not seek resolution to all of life's uncertainties.

Whilst for some the findings in this book may lack credibility, therefore, for others they can seem to contribute to the understanding of ways in which mental health practitioners can help and inspire hope in clients. For some mental health care practitioners this is where some research endeavour needs to be focused.

According to Barker (1997):

> These ways of being with clients which underpin the relationships mental health nurses seek to establish and maintain with clients appear to be under threat from the kind of 'scientism' which has the measure of everything but may fail to appreciate the human importance of anything. (p.18)

Dawson (1997) makes similar remarks, highlighting how the language of nursing, the meaning of care and the subjectivity of spirituality have been suborned by the one-dimensional language of the technocratic society. Consequently, it may be for some that the implicit projection of hope and hopefulness within bereavement counselling is so basic, so bound up with human–human spiritual connection, that it lacks credibility for those concerned with skills acquisition and masculine approaches to care. In a healthcare world more concerned with measurable outcomes, it may be that we have lost sight of such fundamentals. However, as the counsellors and ex-clients in this study pointed out, these subtle, basic yet fundamental social or interpersonal processes appeared to make a key difference in their lives.

Afterword

What comes from the heart, goes to the heart.

Samuel Taylor Coleridge, *Table Talk* (1835)

The relevant theoretical and empirical literature on bereavement counselling is implicit in suggesting a relationship between a completed bereavement reaction and the re-emergence of hope. The emerging substantive grounded theory induced in my study indicates that bereavement counsellors do inspire hope in their clients through an integrated theory comprised of four core variables. An important finding is that this inspiration appears to be a subtle, unobtrusive and implicit process that is bound up with necessary and sufficient human qualities in the counsellor and the projection of these into the environment (and towards the client).

One ex-client in this study described how hope was fundamental to her existence. She stated:

> Hope for me is something deep inside [my heart], a motivation to carry on living. Not just living but living how I want to live.

> Hope for me was about deciding that I wanted to go on.

> Hope would be part of that inner strength. For me an urge, a willingness to continue to live.

Such views of hope chime in with the views of hope expressed in the literature, where hope has been described as 'central' or 'essential'.

However, even though hope appears to have such an important influence on some people's lives, the processes of hope inspiration need to remain subtle and implicit rather than overt. According to Frankl (1959), one cannot be forced to hope: hope cannot be commanded or ordered. Therefore, a theory which suggests that the inspiration of hope is bound up with the presence of certain 'human qualities', and the spiritual connection between clients and counsellors, appears to correspond with Frankl's (1959) views.

As indicated in Chapter 8, in a healthcare world more concerned with measurable outcomes, masculine approaches to care, 'quick fixes' and technological solutions, fundamentals such as human qualities and spiritual connections may be considered as having little value. This is despite the fact that evidence continues to be produced that indicates the value of these fundamentals to healthcare practice (Mental Health Foundation 2000). The absence of simplistic techniques or interventions does not indicate that the counsellor or nurse is powerless to make a difference to a client's life. Yet, if, as Frankl pointed out, hope cannot be forced, commanded or ordered, perhaps practitioners should be more concerned with the 'human' aspects of practice. The Dalai Lama (1998) makes similar remarks:

> There is no way that you can come up with one or two simple techniques that can solve all problems – however it is helpful to understand and appreciate the importance of compassion in human relationships and empathy. (p.91)

He goes on later to say:

> But then there's another level of spirituality. This is what I call basic spirituality, basic human qualities of goodness, kindness, compassion and caring… But as long as we are human beings, as long as we are all members of the human family, all of us need these basic human values. Without these, human existence becomes very hard, very dry. (p.307)

Therefore, perhaps practitioners need to be mindful of Samuel Taylor Coleridge's statement quoted at the start of this chapter. If practitioners wish to enspirit another person's heart; to inspire hope in others, they should begin by first looking to their own heart, and implicitly projecting their hope into the other person. Thus, when considering the inspiration of hope, practitioners would be prudent to remember that the most powerful 'tool' at their disposal to aid them in this process is themselves.

Summary of the Research

Grounded theory

The theory of the inspiration of hope in bereavement counselling that forms the basis of this book was developed from my own research with bereavement counsellors and ex-clients. The research method used was that of grounded theory (Glaser and Strauss 1967) – an analytical strategy for dealing with and making sense of unstructured qualitative data, and for generating theory from the data. The inspection and analysis of qualitative data generates emergent theory through a process of categorising the data and making linkages between categories at various levels of abstraction. Phyllis Stern (1980), one of the earliest nurse scholars to use the grounded-theory method, describes the process of inducing a theory using the grounded method as one comprising five stages:

1. Collection of empirical data – the researcher collects data from interviews, observations, documents or from a combination of these sources.

2. Concept formation – a tentative conceptual framework is generated from the categorisation of the data.

3. Concept development – the tentative framework and the emerging theory are developed by grouping categories in linked clusters, sampling the existing literature, and adding data for comparison to refine and consolidate the categories; 'sub-core variables' begin to emerge.

4. Concept modification and integration – the emerging theory is more fully integrated and delimited; concepts are compared with more highly developed concepts, and these are compared with more data; the researcher should become empirically confident of the identity and nature of the core variable (see below).

5. Production of a research report.

Criteria for establishing a core variable (Glaser 1978)

- It must be central – that is, related to as many other categories and their properties as possible and more than other candidates for the core category. The criteria of centrality is a necessary condition to make it core.
- It must recur frequently in the data. By its frequent recurrence it comes to be seen as a stable pattern and becomes more and more related to other variables.
- By being more related to many other categories and reoccurring frequently, it takes more time to saturate the core category than other categories.
- It relates meaningfully and easily with other categories. These connections are not forced, rather their realization comes quick and richly.
- It has clear and grabbing implication for formal theory.
- It has clear and considerable carry-through in that it does not lead to dead ends in theory or leave the analyst high and dry.
- It is completely variable in that its frequent relations to other categories makes it highly variable in degree, dimension and type. It is readily modifiable through these dependent variations.
- It is also a dimension of the problem. Thus, it in part explains itself and its own variations.

Data collection and concept formation

Data for the study were collected during in-depth interviews. It was thought that this would provide the best opportunity for following particular avenues of inquiry, for responding to apparent key issues and topics, and for establishing the degree of rapport necessary to enable participants to offer the most in-depth explanation of the processes being studied.

Initially six interviews were held. After each interview came the process of the tentative labelling of the phenomena that the interviewer had perceived. This was achieved by dealing with the material in the transcripts paragraph by paragraph. Starting with the first paragraph these questions were asked:

What do we have here?

What categories, concepts or do we need in order to describe or to account for the phenomena discussed in this paragraph? (see Turner 1981)

The analysis of the first six interviews produced 36 tentative conceptual categories:

1. the process of establishing a relationship
2. trust and belief
3. hearing and understanding the client
4. conveying acceptance
5. establishing safety and trust
6. testing out the counsellor
7. following the client's pace and tone
8. balancing within the counsellor
9. dichotomy of bereavement
10. accessing the pain
11. stillness
12. challenge defences and blind areas
13. the dark side
14. touch/no touch
15. working with images
16. talking about the negative
17. providing support
18. the therapist's felt sense
19. external supervision
20. the therapist's hope
21. implicit, inextricable hope
22. traces of hope in the client (nurturing the seed)
23. client's hopelessness
24. the re-emergence of hope: forward orientation, increased activation
25. working toward an ending
26. tasks of grieving
27. off-loading baggage
28. interventions to promote reflection
29. client's personal attributes
30. reflecting on the positive
31. early experiences
32. growth of awareness in the client
33. the therapist's genuineness
34. the therapist's commitment and tenacity
35. avoiding colluding with the client
36. modelling a healthy response.

Table A.1 The research sample

Interviewee No.1	Male psychotherapist and educationalist Operates predominantly using a psychodynamic approach to bereavement counselling Practising as a therapist for over 10 years
Interviewee No.2	Female clinical nurse specialist/psychotherapist Operates solely using a psychodynamic approach to bereavement counselling Practising as a therapist for over 15 years
Interviewee No.3	Female psychotherapist Operates predominantly using a humanistic approach to bereavement counselling Practising as a therapist for over 10 years
Interviewee No.4	Male clinical nurse specialist/psychotherapist Operates solely using a gestalt approach to bereavement counselling Practising as a therapist for over 15 years.
Interviewee No.5	Male psychotherapist and educationalist Operates solely using a person-centred approach to bereavement counselling Practising as a therapist for over 8 years
Interviewee No.6	Male psychotherapist and educationalist Operates mainly using an eclectic approach to bereavement counselling Practising as a therapist for over 8 years
Interviewee No.7	Female psychotherapist Operates solely using a person-centred approach to bereavement counselling Practising as a therapist for over 15 years
Interviewee No.8	Male psychotherapist and educationalist Operates mainly using an eclectic approach, with an emphasis on person-centred work, to bereavement counselling Practising as a therapist for over 15 years
Interviewee No.9	Female ex-client Received bereavement counselling following the death of her mother
Interviewee No.10	Male ex-client Received bereavement counselling following the death of his father
Interviewee No.11	Female ex-client Received bereavement counselling following the death of her child
Interviewee No.12	Male ex-client Received bereavement counselling following the death of his mother

Concept development

This stage involves reducing the categories by discovering 'umbrella terms' under which several categories fit, in that each category is now compared with the other categories to see how they cluster or connect. The umbrella term can thus be seen to encompass several initial labels. It may be worth pointing out that after conducting only six interviews at this point, many of the links and connections are tenuous and need further exploration in subsequent interviews. Furthermore, the sub-core and core variables are given only tentative, provisional names that indicate something of the emerging processes.

The tentative sub-core variables are:

- forming a relationship (Table A.2)
- releasing pain (Table A.3)
- a good ending (Table A.4).

The tentative core variable:

- implicit hope (Table A.5).

Table A.2 Tentative sub-core variable composition: Forming a relationship	
1	The process of establishing a relationship
3	Hearing and understanding the client
4	Conveying acceptance
7	Following the client's pace and tone
2	Trust and belief within the counsellor
8	Balance within the counsellor
6	Testing out the counsellor
33	The therapist's genuiness
34	The therapist's commitment and tenacity
13	The dark side
5	Establishing a sense of safety and trust

Table A.3 Tentative sub-core variable composition: Releasing pain

10	Accessing the pain
17	Providing support
12	Challenging defences and blind areas
28	Interventions to promote reflection
14	Touch, no touch
11	Stillness
18	The therapist's felt sense
27	Off-loading baggage
16	Talking about the negative
15	Working with images
35	Avoiding colluding with the client
9	The dichotomy of bereavement

Table A.4 Tentative sub-core variable composition: A good ending

36	Modelling a healthy response
25	Working towards an ending
22	Traces of hope in the client (nurturing the seed)
23	Client's hopelessness
31	Early experiences
29	Client's personal attributes
26	Tasks of grieving
30	Reflecting on the positive
32	Growth of awareness in the client
24	The re-emergence of hope

Table A.5 Tentative core variable composition: Implicit hope	
21	Implicit, inextricable hope
20	The therapist's hope
19	External supervision

At this stage in the research it was starting to become apparent that this core variable could be regarded as the hub of the theory of the inspiration of hope within bereavement counselling. Or, to phrase this in another way, this was starting to look like the key basic psychosocial process, or interpersonal process of hope inspiration. There are five reasons for suggesting this emerging centrality:

1. The presence and influence of hope within the bereavement counselling was ever-present. As long as the counsellor had hope, this hope was involved in the process. In contrast to the sub-core variables (forming a relationship, releasing pain and a good ending) the processes captured by this core variable were not restricted to one stage or phase. From the very first to the very last session, the counsellor needed to have hope and to be able to project hopefulness. If the counsellor is receiving regular, high-quality clinical supervision in order to sustain and replenish their hope, then this hope can be used in the therapy. Similarly, most (if not all) bereavement counsellors will be receiving regular supervision before the client commences his/her therapy. They will continue to receive this supervision throughout the therapy and will go on receiving supervision when the therapy has finished. Hence, each of the categories in this core variable (the implicit, inextricable hope, the therapist's hope and external supervision) are present all the way through the therapy and thus can be regarded as ever-present rather than linear.

2. The implicit nature of hope inspiration was indicated by the data, in that it was bound up with practices and interventions that have been explained in each of the preceding sub-core variables. Furthermore, this core variable provides the answer.

3. Since each of the preceding sub-core variables alluded to the implicit nature of hope inspiration, they could be subsumed within this larger, more encompassing core variable.

4. This was the last core variable that appeared to reach saturation. The researcher has achieved category saturation when 'no additional data are being found whereby the sociologist can develop properties of the

category' (Glaser and Strauss 1967, p.61); that is, when similar instances recur over and over again.

5.   This core variable alludes to the centrality of implicit hope to the process of hope inspiration in bereavement counselling. Each of the processes described and explained in the preceding sub-core variables required the presence of hope within the therapy (and therapist) in order to be effective.

Because this is the core variable identified in the bereavement counselling process, it is worth describing in greater detail the categories it embraces using some of the actual recorded interviewee statements.

The first category in this core variable is *Implicit, inextricable hope*. The counsellors described how the atmosphere or environment within the therapy was a hopeful one. This category appears to have two properties. The first property is concerned with (despite dealing with issues which are synonymous with hopelessness or despair) the counsellor bringing a sense of hope and hopefulness into the therapy (and he/she was able to continue to bring this hope as a result of having his/her own hope replenished in his/her clinical supervision); however, this hope was not expressed overtly. The second property is concerned with the counsellor's implicit hope in the person's capability to acknowledge his/her pain, express this pain, to experience the bereavement, deal with the emotions, and then reach a more hopeful position: for example, the hope that the client could even grow as a result of the experience. Counsellors described how hope was around in the therapy, but that the word was seldom used: it was more to do with being present in the atmosphere. This was described by the interviewees in the following ways:

> It is an implicit message of hope that I convey, by believing that given the right environment, and time, they will overcome this. (Int. 5)

> Even when the person is communicating their sense of hopelessness, just by being there physically communicates a sense that all is not lost, that there is hope, that I, the therapist doesn't believe it is hopeless. (Int. 6)

> I didn't focus on inspiring or instilling hope, it was bound up, implicit. (Int. 1)

> I project my hope into the situation at a very basic or fundamental level just by my willingness to work with the client. (Int. 5)

The second category in this core variable is *The therapist's hope*. This category appears to contain three properties. Counsellors spoke of having a sense of hope in themselves, their ability and in their decisions, so the first property is concerned with this hope. The second property is concerned with the projection of this hope to the client. The third property is concerned with the counsellors not 'taking on board' any sense of hopelessness that the client projected. Many authors have alluded to the emotional transference that can occur in a counselling setting. This is most often explained in terms of the feelings the counsellors pick up (or inherit) from the client. Counsellors may end a session with a certain feeling and not know why they are feeling this way. The same transference of feelings can occur from counsellor to client, and in this case the counsellor can transfer or project his/her own sense of hope to the client. This was not carried out in an overt sense and indeed counsellors are not overtly buoyant or 'over the top'. This was captured by one of the counsellors who stated:

> I never say to the client 'Things will be fine one day', but I do have a belief and hope that they can reach a point where they will be OK. (Int. 4)

Counsellors were quite clear about how they projected hope. This was described by the interviewees in the following ways:

> I inspire hope by believing in me, believing that I can offer something. (Int. 5)

> I inspire hope by never giving up on the client. (Int. 5)

> The person that is responsible for bringing hope into the session is the counsellor. (Int. 5)

> I model a sense of hopefulness that things will change over time. (Int. 4)

The fourth property is concerned with the hope counsellors have in the process and in the theoretical underpinnings of the approach they utilized. One interviewee described this in the following way:

> I had hope in the core conditions, that they would be enough. (Int. 5)

With regard to the first property, this hope in themselves was particularly evident when the counsellors had to take a risk. At times the counsellors would experience a sense of intrapersonal conflict with their hearts saying one thing and their heads saying another. For example, sometimes when challenging a particular defence or denial, the counsellors had to hope that not colluding with the client would ultimately be in the client's best interest. Even though this would mean emotional pain for both the client and the counsellor, in effect, they took a risk and hoped that they were doing the right thing.

This category, *External supervision*, has two properties and the links between these and the preceding categories indicate why it belongs in this core variable. The first property is concerned with the renewal or replenishment of the counsellor's hope by means of the supervision they receive. No individual has a limitless resource of hope, yet as the data in this study have indicated, the person responsible for bringing hope to the therapy is the counsellor. If, as this theory posits, the counsellor's hope is being projected into another person and is consequently being used to sustain two people, it will be depleted more quickly than if it were being used to sustain just one person. If this depletion of hope levels continues unchecked, the counsellor will reach a point where they are no longer able to bring any hope into the therapy, and the therapist will have no hope to project onto the client. As previously indicated, the counsellor's hope appears to be central to the entire basic process of hope inspiration within bereavement counselling – hence the requirement for the counsellor to have his/her own hope resource 'topped up' during clinical supervision. How this actually happens is outside the remit of this research but is clearly one of the next logical questions that needs to be asked and researched. This was described by the interviewees in the following ways:

> I get a sense of hope from my supervision. (Int. 1)

> The external supervisor can inject some hope based on all their experience. (Int. 4)

> I get my hope through my external supervision. (Int. 4)

> My own hope is sustained and replenished by my own therapy and my own clinical supervision. (Int. 5)

> I maintain my own hope through my own supervision. It is a ritual for me, that supervision be exploited at all times. (Int. 6)

The second property is concerned with the risks taken by the counsellor within the therapy, as these are subsequently checked out and explored (and verified) in supervision. This was described by one of the interviewees in the following way:

> In supervision we explore and unravel the dynamics of the bereavement counselling and from that several hopeful or hope inspiring thoughts and feelings become apparent. (Int. 6)

Concept modification and integration

In this stage the integrated theoretical framework is postulated. The tenuous theoretical links and connections already identified are further explored in subsequent interviews.

The results of this stage of the research suggested modification of both the content and the labelling of the sub-core and core variables.

The sub-core variables are:

- forging the connection and relationship (Table A.6)
- facilitating a cathartic release (Table A.7)
- experiencing a health [good] ending (Table A.8).

The core variable:

- implicit projection of hope and hopefulness (Table A.9).

As indicated in the initial discussion of this core variable, the implicit projection of hope and hopefulness appears to be the core or central aspect of this theory, in that all the other categories and sub-core variables are linked to it and could be subsumed

Table A.6 Sub-core variable: Forging the connection and relationship

Experiencing a caring, human–human connection

Countering the projection of hopelessness

Unwavering commitment

Rediscovering trust

Permeating hope throughout the counselling encounter

Table A.7 Sub-core variable: Facilitating a cathartic release

Facilitating the release of painful emotion

Supplying the opportunity for reflection

Providing unconditional and continual support

Freeing the client to talk about the deceased

Employing therapeutic touch

Purposefully using silence

Avoiding colluding with the client's denial and/or hopelessness

Table A.8 Sub-core variable: Experiencing a healthy [good] ending

Realising the potential for growth in bereavement

Avoiding repeats

Accomplishing any tasks of bereavement

Ensuring clients retain control

Increasing the client's self-awareness

Table A.9 Core variable: The implicit projection of hope and hopefulness

Implicit, inextricable hope

The therapist's hope

External supervision

within this core variable (see Figure 2.1). The data collected from the counsellors always appeared to indicate that a sense of hope and hopefulness permeated the whole process of the bereavement counselling. Similarly, the ex-clients who were interviewed described how they were more hopeful following the completion of therapy than they were prior to the therapy. However, these interviewees also commented that, despite the constant presence and influence of hope, it was very rarely referred to explicitly. Furthermore, the interviewees described how, when the counsellors introduced their own explicit hope or agenda into the therapy, this became counterproductive. Hence, there is a continual sense of hope for the counsellor, and this is introduced, implicitly, into each encounter with the clients, and at the conclusion of the therapy the clients possess some of this hope for themselves. This core variable indicates that hope is inspired by the implicit projection of hope and hopefulness through a combination of the three categories listed in Table 7.9 and explained in more detail below.

Comparing new labels with existing labels and categories, enabled the categories to undergo further modification and refinement. As a result the name of the core variable was amended, although its composition remained the same.

As indicated in the initial discussion, this core variable is about the counsellors' sense of hope and hopefulness, and how this was projected into the therapy and towards the client. It also refers to the importance of clinical supervision as one method of restoring and sustaining the therapist's hope. Many authors have alluded to the emotional transference that can occur in a counselling setting (Pearlman and Saakvitine 1995; Shur 1994).

Despite the absence of any literature that made specific reference to hope in bereavement counselling, counsellors were adamant that they had hope, that this hope was brought into the therapy session, and that it was projected into the client. This was well captured by the counsellors who stated:

> I hope that one of the things I would provide, is to give them some hope. (Int. 8)

> You project some of your own hopefulness? Yes, very much so. (Int. 8)

> I have a fundamental belief and hope that what I am doing is good. I believe in the value of therapy, and I believe I do my job better because I have this belief, this hope. (Int. 8)

> My hope exists, and I know it exists because I am a very hopeful person. (Int. 7)

> My hope is that people naturally want to hope. People naturally want to move on. (Int. 7)

The core variable is also concerned with the implicit, inextricable and yet central nature of hope inspiration within bereavement counselling. Furthermore, the counsellors identified the problems that could arise from an overt attempt by the counsellors to inspire hope in the clients. Such overt hopefulness was described as an imposition of the counsellors' agenda which would do little to help the client feel and experience more hope and hopefulness. This was expressed by the interviewees in the following ways:

> The counselling situation provides the framework for the inspiration of hope to occur. (Int. 8)

> Hope inspiration is implicit. When it becomes a projection of the counsellor's agenda, then it can become counterproductive. (Int. 7)

> The hope re-emerges naturally, as a result of the appropriate environment. (Int. 7)

> My hope inspiration is quite implicit and bound up and I think this illustrates a difference between experienced and inexperienced counsellors. (Int. 7)

> Actually, if you say it explicitly [hope] it does more harm than good. But its like this, its only by having that hope that you can stay with the absolute horror and despair. (Int. 7)

> Hope inspiration maybe so bound up in the counsellor's demeanour, the counsellor's manner and in certain qualities they convey. (Int. 7)

When asked: 'If it's implicit, how do you know it is going on?', the counsellor replied:

> Because they [the clients] tell me. Clients say things, they will start to talk about what happens next. They are verbal about what is happening to them. Also, they change physically. You can see them re-engaging with life. They look forward to what is happening. (Int. 7)

In addition to the evidence provided by the counsellors that they had hope and projected hope into the therapy, the ex-clients described their experience of hope in the bereavement counselling. The data provided by the ex-clients and subsequent theoretical memos appeared to indicate that the emotional atmosphere within the bereavement counselling contained a strong element of hope and hopefulness. Throughout the process of data collection and analysis, the following issues were borne in mind:

- If hope is present in the atmosphere, who brings it?
- Whose responsibility is it to ensure it is there?
- Do the counsellors have hope and if so, what is the nature of this hope?
- The counsellors have hope, so they introduce it into the atmosphere somehow.
- Hope needs to remain implicit, otherwise it can be damaging, therefore the therapist's hope has to be introduced into the atmosphere implicitly.

The data provided by the ex-clients added to this questioning and theorising. The ex-clients became very much aware that hope did permeate the atmosphere within the therapy, but they confirmed that it remained implicit. Indeed, the word was seldom used. Yet, the ex-clients sensed that their counsellors were hopeful, that they had their own hope, that they had hope in the client's potential, hope in the spirit or potential of human beings and hope in the process and value of therapy. The presence, influence and projection of the therapist's implicit hope was described by the ex-clients in the following ways:

> We worked in a very hopeful atmosphere. (Int. 11)

> I think the concept of hope was around, but I don't have recollections that we used the word. But it was more to do with being present in the 'atmosphere'. (Int. 11)

> My therapist was a very hopeful person. (Int. 10)

> My therapist had hope. (Int. 11)

> My therapist had hope in the human process. He was hopeful that, yes, as human beings I/we can do this. It was hope in me as a human being. (Int. 10)

> I think it is the therapist's responsibility to bring some hope. (Int. 11)

> I certainly got a sense that the counsellor had hope, that she was a hopeful person. (Int. 9)

> The therapist brings that hope to the relationship. (Int. 11)

> He had hope that given the right environment and conditions I would be able to come through this. (Int. 10)

> The therapist recognized that he was just one source of hope. One component in the larger whole of the help I was getting. (Int. 11)

The projection of hope and hopefulness may perhaps be thought of, or can be likened to, a transplantation of the hope resource from the counsellor to the client. This projection of hope appears to have at least two processes. The first is concerned with an indirect, osmosis-like process. The therapy takes place in an environment where hope is present, in that it is projected, implicitly, into the environment by the counsellor. Consequently, this emotional atmosphere gradually permeates and conveys itself to the client. Our emotional selves are not immune from the emotional environment in which we exist. In the same way as a sponge or blotting paper, the individual can soak up the emotional atmosphere. The second process is concerned with a more direct, although still implicit, process. Given the theory that souls touch during such care, it is reasonable to suggest that this is one way that hope is projected or transplanted from the counsellor to the client. This caring, this transpersonal connection, allows hope to flow from one person to another, particularly in the spiritual dimension of self. In the first sub-core variable, *forming a relationship*, a connection or relationship was forged between the client and counsellor. This connection or relationship existed on several levels, or had a multidimensional nature. Consequently, one such connection occurred within the spiritual dimension. The ex-clients made reference to this spiritual connection and expressed it in the following ways:

> I would leave the therapy perhaps feeling more alive, some feeling of being connected, something had been validated by the therapist. (Int. 11)

> There was a spiritual engagement between us. (Int. 11)

> There is a spiritual connection and intimacy between the therapist and me, that is definitely there. (Int. 10)

> As a result of the therapy, the spiritual engagement, something had developed and changed. (Int. 11)

> The spiritual connection has to do with the connectedness, the trusting that is established. That they connect with me, and I with them at many levels. (Int. 10)

> The spiritual connection is about, even though I may not be able to use words, they can still understand me, or can have contact with me. (Int. 10)

Perhaps the potential for the inspiration (or projection) of hope from the counsellor to the client as a result of the spiritual connection that exists was best captured by one of the ex-clients who stated:

> In this spiritual connection it is possible that I can pick up on what the therapist is feeling and he can pick up on what I am feeling. (Int. 10)

Establishing the credibility of the findings

Glaser and Strauss (1967) indicate that, in order for a grounded theory to have practical application, whether substantive or formal, the theory needs to have four highly interrelated properties. These properties are summarized under the headings 'fitness', 'understanding', 'generality' and 'control'.

To establish the credibility of the grounded theory of the inspiration of hope in bereavement counselling, the following arrangements were made:

1. When the theory was considered to be complete, each of the interviewees was contacted and an appointment made.
2. The interviewee was informed that the purpose of this meeting was to attempt to establish the credibility of the theory.
3. The interviewee was invited to view the transcript of the original interview.

4. Glaser's four properties for determining the credibility of a grounded theory were explained to the interviewee.
5. The theory of hope inspiration within bereavement counselling was explained; interviewees were asked to consider the merit of the theory with respect to each of the four properties.
6. The interviewee was invited to ask questions and raise queries.
7. These comments were recorded on paper in full view of the interviewee.
8. These comments and feedback were then tabulated (see Table A.10).

I have previously outlined the procedure for establishing the credibility of the emerging theory (see Chapter 4). Table A.10 illustrates the interviewee responses to the author's questions regarding the fit, workability (understandability), generality and control of the emerging theory. I managed to obtain these comments from all but one of the interviewees (Int. 3). Additionally, the ex-clients were not asked questions concerning the generality (and adaptability) or control of the theory. These not applicable areas are marked as N/A in the table.

Some additional points and questions raised by the interviewees were:

- Is everyone appropriate for bereavement counselling?
- The person's pre-bereavement personality may influence the outcome.
- Where does the 'germ of hope' come from?
- It can't be a one-way linear process all the time.
- I would describe the re-emergence of hope being like the tide coming in, in waves. It gradually moves forward, but it also moves back and forwards too.

Examination of the interviewee feedback comments regarding the four criteria for establishing the credibility of a grounded theory appears to suggest that the emerging theory can be considered to be credible, for this group of people, at this particular point in time.

No interviewee suggested that the theory has no fit or 'grab', and nothing in the theory struck them as being particularly out of place.

All the interviewees stated that they could understand the theory and the counsellors stated that they could use it in practice. However, one counsellor mentioned that she was uncomfortable with some of the language (e.g. the word 'collude').

Those counsellors that had anything to say about the generality of the theory said that they could adapt the theory as necessary. Similarly, those counsellors that had anything to say about control said the theory reinforced their current practice (i.e. giving control back to the client), it could provide intentionality to their work, and might be particularly useful for less experienced counsellors.

Table A.10 Interviewee responses regarding the properties of the emerging theory

	Fitness	Understanding	Generality	Control
Int. 1	Brilliant, it fits.	Yes.	I could use this as my practice evolves.	It confirms my position on giving clients the control.
Int. 2	Yes. It's good.	Yes, I understand it.	Yes, this looks flexible enough for me to use it with a variety of clients.	Yes, it could provide a degree of control.
Int. 3	N/A	N/A	N/A	N/A
Int. 4	Very accurate.	I would go along with this completely.	I think so.	Not sure.
	Fitness	Understanding	Generality	Control
Int. 5	Absolutely.	Yes, completely.	Hope is more widespread and involved than most people would agree.	Yes, I think it could.
Int. 6	Sounds OK to me. Phase 1 might be separated into 1a and 1b?	I think it is interesting what you have come up with. I maybe have some problems with the language.	It could be adapted. It is general enough to be adaptable.	It gives me control in that it provides purpose and intentionality to my practice, and provides the underpinning theory.
Int. 7	It is logical. The sequence fits. It has both process and content issues. A good fluid way.	Yes I understand it. It is not entirely unlike things that already exist.	It is an important starting point. More applicable to longer-term work.	It does show less experienced counsellors that they don't always have to be in control.

Continued on next page...

Table A.10 continued

	Fitness	**Understanding**	**Generality**	**Control**
Int. 8	It definitely fits.	Yes, I understand it. I think it makes sense.	I could use this.	It may help less experienced counsellors more.
Int. 9	Yes.	Yes.	N/A	N/A
Int. 10	I really go along with the spiritual connection. That's the bit that really brought me back to life.	Wonderful. The modelling of a healthy ending is very useful. Don't like the term 'dark side'.	I haven't read anything as detailed as this.	N/A
Int. 11	I would go along completely. If someone is overt, I wouldn't believe it.	Yes, I understand it.	N/A	N/A

Category saturation

Theoretical sampling within grounded theory does not cease once a predetermined number of sample units have been accessed. Theoretical sampling ceases once the categories are saturated. It follows that, if a researcher ceases data collection and analysis prior to saturating the theory and categories, then the resulting theory can be criticized for being incomplete. A key question facing a researcher using a grounded theory method is therefore: 'Have I achieved saturation of my categories and theory?'

Glaser and Strauss (1967) point out that the researcher has achieved category saturation when no additional data are being found from which the sociologist can develop properties of the category. Thus, when the researcher sees similar instances occurring over and over again, the researcher becomes empirically confident that he has saturated his categories.

A further 'test' to determine whether or not saturation has been achieved was carried out during my attempts to establish the credibility of the theory. An extra question put to each of the interviewees was:

Is there anything that strikes you as missing from the theory? Are there any glaringly obvious omissions or holes in the theory?

If any of the interviewees stated that concept 'X' or process 'Y' was missing from the theory, this might suggest unsaturated categories and therefore an incomplete theory. Table A.11 displays the interviewees' responses to this question; however, it is important to note that, as stated previously, grounded theory can be seen as process, in that a grounded theory is never complete (Glaser and Strauss 1967). As it is applied and explained, the theory becomes an ever developing entity and can evolve continuously (Glaser 1992). Therefore, even if all the interviewees indicate that the categories and theory appear to be saturated, it may not be prudent to regard the theory as complete. Inversely, if any interviewees suggest that saturation may not have occurred in all the categories, whilst these apparent omissions should be made clear, their presence does not indicate that the theory cannot develop or evolve into a useful and applicable theory. A saturated grounded theory made up of saturated categories does represent the most complete theory possible for that substantive (or formal) group at that particular moment in time.

Table A.11 Interviewee responses regarding category saturation	
Int. 1	Nothing obvious is missing.
Int. 2	
Int. 3	
Int. 4	I can't think of anything that is jarringly missing.
Int. 5	I can't think of anything.
Int. 6	Not at the moment.
Int. 7	No.
Int. 8	I don't think so.
Int. 9	No.
Int. 10	Nothing strikes me.
Int. 11	I would see the cyclic process within the linear process as a wave-like process. You know, how the tide moves in gradually.

References

Aldridge, D. (1998) *Suicide: The Tragedy of Hopelessness*. London: Jessica Kingsley Publishers.

Altschul, A. (1997) 'A personal view of psychiatric nursing.' In S. Tilley (ed) *The Mental Health Nurse: Views of Practice and Education*. London: Blackwell Science. 1–14.

Argyle, M. (1975) *Bodily Communication*. London: Metheun.

Barker, P. (1997) 'Towards a meta-theory of psychiatric nursing practice.' *Mental Health Practice 1*, 4, 18–21.

Barker, P. (1999a) *The Philosophy and Practice of Psychiatric Nursing*. Edinburgh: Churchill Livingstone.

Barker, P. (1999b) 'The healing of the mind.' In P. Barker (ed) *The Talking Cures: A Guide to the Psychotherapies for Healthcare Professionals*. London: Nursing Times Books. 7–21.

Barker, P. and Kerr, B. (2001) *The Process of Psychotherapy: A Journey of Discovery*. Oxford: Butterworth Heinemann.

Barker, P., Reynolds, B. and Stevenson, C. (1997) 'The human science basis of psychiatric nursing: theory and practice.' *Journal of Advanced Nursing 25*, 660–667.

Barkham, M. (1996) 'Individual therapy: Process and outcome findings across successive research generations.' In W. Dryden (ed) *Handbook of Individual Therapy* (3rd edn). London: Sage. 328–364.

Barnard, D. (1995) 'Chronic illness and the dynamics of hoping.' In S.K. Toombs, D. Barnard and R.A. Carson (eds) *Chronic Illness: From Experience to Policy*. Indianapolis: Indianallumni Press. 38–57.

Beech, P. and Norman, I.J. (1995) 'Patients' perceptions of the quality of psychiatric nursing care: Findings from a small-scale descriptive study.' *Journal of Clinical Nursing 4*, 117–123.

Benner, P. (1984) *From Novice to Expert: Excellence and Power in Clinical Practice*. New York: Addison-Wesley.

Benner, P. and Wrubel, J. (1989) *The Primacy of Caring: Stress and Coping in Health and Illness*. New York: Addison Wesley.

Brown, M. and Fowler, G. (1979) *Psychodynamic Nursing: A BioSocial Orientation*. Philadelphia: W.B. Saunders.

Bruss, C.R. (1988) 'Nursing diagnosis of hopelessness.' *Journal of Psychosocial Nursing 26*, 3, 18–21.

Campbell, P. (1997) 'Listening to patients.' In P. Barker and B. Davidson (eds) *Psychiatric Nursing: Ethical Strife*. London: Arnold. 237–248.

Carter, S.L. (1989) 'Themes of grief.' *Nursing Research 38*, 6, 354–358.

Chambers, M. (1998) 'Mental health nursing: The challenge of evidence based practice.' *Mental Health Practice 1*, 8, 18–22.

Clarke, L. (1999) *Challenging Ideas in Psychiatric Nursing*. London: Routledge.

Crow, H.E. (1991) 'How to help patients understand and conquer grief: Avoiding depression in the midst of sadness.' *Postgraduate Medicine 89*, 8, 117–118, 121–122.

Cutcliffe, J.R. (1995) 'How do nurses inspire and instil hope in terminally ill HIV patients?' *Journal of Advanced Nursing 22*, 888–895.

Cutcliffe, J.R. (1996) 'Critically ill patients' perspectives of hope.' *British Journal of Nursing 5*, 11, 674, 687–690.

Cutcliffe, J.R. (1998) 'Is psychiatric nursing research barking up the wrong tree?' *Nurse Education Today 18*, 257–258.

Cutcliffe, J.R., Dikintis, J., Carberry, J., Tilley, C., Turner, S., Anderson-Moll, D. and Cooper, W. (1997) 'Users' views of their continuing care community psychiatric services.' *The International Journal of Psychiatric Nursing Research 3*, 3, 382–394.

Cutcliffe, J.R. and Goward, P. (2000) 'Mental health nurses and qualitative research methods: A mutual attraction?' *Journal of Advanced Nursing 31*, 3, 590–598.

Cutcliffe, J.R. and Grant, G. (2001) 'What are the principles and processes of inspiring hope in cognitively impaired older adults within a continuing care environment?' *Journal of Psychiatric and Mental Health Nursing 8*, 5, 427–436.

Dalai Lama and Cutler, H.C. (1998) *The Art of Happiness: A Handbook for Living.* Sydney: Hodder.

Dawson, P.J. (1997) 'Thoughts of a wet mind in a dry season: the rhetoric and ideology of psychiatric nursing.' *Nursing Inquiry 4*, 69–71.

Dickoff, J. and James, P. (1968) 'A theory of theories: A position paper.' *Nursing Research 17*, 197–203.

DiGiulio, J.F. (1992) 'Early widowhood: An atypical transition.' *Journal of Mental Health Counselling (Special Issue: Women and Health) 14*, 1, 97–109.

Drew, B.L. (1990) 'Differentiation of hopelessness, helplessness and powerlessness using Erickson's "Roots of virtue".' *Archives of Psychiatric Nursing 4*, 5, 332–337.

Duck, S. (1992) *Human Relationships* (2nd edn). London: Sage.

DuFault, K. and Martocchio, B.C. (1985) 'Hope – its spheres and dimensions.' In K. DuFault and B.C. Martocchio (eds) *Nursing Clinics of North America 20*, 2, 379–391.

Elbeck, M. and Fecteau, G. (1990) 'Improving the validity of measures of patient satisfaction with psychiatric care and treatment.' *Hospital and Community Psychiatry 41*, 9, 998–1001.

English National Board for Nurses, Midwives and Health Visitors (1997) *Standards for Approval of Higher Education Institutions and Programmes.* London: ENB.

Erickson, E.H. (1964) *Childhood and Society* (2nd edn). New York: WW Norton.

Farran, C., Salloway, J.C. and Clark, D.C. (1990) 'Measurement of hope in a community based older population.' *Western Journal of Nursing Research 12*, 1, 42–59.

Frankl, V. (1959) *Man's Search for Meaning.* London: Hodder and Stoughton.

Glaser, B. and Strauss, A.L. (1967) *The Discovery of Grounded Theory: Strategies for Qualitative Research.* Chicago: Aldine.

Glaser, B.G. (1978) *Theoretical Sensitivity: Advances in the Methodology of Grounded Theory.* Mill Valley California: Sociology Press.

Glaser, B.G. (1992) *Basics of Grounded Theory Analysis.* Mill Valley, California: Sociology Press.

Glick, I.O., Weiss, R.S. and Parkes, C.M. (1974) *The First Year of Bereavement.* New York: Wiley.

Gordon, D., Alexander, D.A. and Dietzan, J. (1979) 'The psychiatric patient: A voice to be heard.' *British Journal of Psychiatry 135*, 115–121.

Harvey, J.H., Orbuch, T.L., Weber, A.L. and Merbach, N. (1992) 'House of pain and hope: Accounts of pain and loss.' *Death Studies 16*, 99–124.

Herth, K. (1990a) 'Fostering hope in terminally ill people.' *Journal of Advanced Nursing 15*, 1250–1259.

Hill, B. and Micheal, S. (1996) 'The Human factor.' *Journal of Psychiatric and Mental Health Nursing 3*, 245–248.

Hinds, P. (1984) 'Inducing a definition of hope through the use of grounded theory.' *Journal of Advanced Nursing 9*, 4, 357–362.

Holms, T.H. and Rahe, R.H. (1967) 'The social readjustment rating scale.' *Journal of Psychosomatic Research 11.*

Kubler-Ross, E. (1970) *On Death and Dying.* London: Tavistock.

Kuhn, T.S. (1962) The Structure of the Scientific Revolutions 1st Edition. Chicago: University of Chicago Press.

Kylma, J. and Vehvilainen-Julkunen, K. (1997) 'Hope in nursing research: A meta-analysis of the ontological and epistemological foundations of research on hope.' *Journal of Advanced Nursing 25,* 364–371.

Landrum, P.A. (1993) 'Philosophical positions.' In Rawlins, Williams and Beck (eds) *Mental Health Nursing – A Holistic Life Cycle Approach.* Philadelphia: Mosby. 40–52.

Lego, S. (1998) 'Managed care of outpatient psychiatry – a new twist: Perspectives in psychiatric care.' *The Journal for Nurse Psychotherapists 35,* 1, 1.

Lego, S. (1999) 'Commentary: Psychoanalysis and psychiatric nursing.' In P. Barker (1999) *The Philosophy and Practice of Psychiatric Nursing.* Edinburgh: Churchill Livingstone.

Leick, N. and Davidsen-Nielson, M. (1987) *Healing Pain: Attachment, Loss and Grief Therapy.* London: Routledge.

Lendrum, S. and Syme, G. (1992) *Gift of Tears: A Practical Approach to Loss and Bereavement Counselling.* London: Routledge.

Lynch, W.F. (1965) *Images of Hope.* Baltimore: Garamony/Trichemah.

McIntyre, K., Farrell, M. and David, A. (1989) 'In-patient psychiatric care: The patient's view.' *British Journal of Medical Psychology 62,* 249–255.

McKenna, H. (1997) *Nursing Theories and Models.* London: Routledge.

Marcel, G.G. (1948) in H.J. Blackham (1986) *Six Existentialist Thinkers.* London: Routledge. 140–159.

Mental Health Foundation (2000) *Strategies for Living.* London: Mental Health Foundation.

Michael, S. (1994) 'Invisible skills.' *Journal of Psychiatric and Mental Health Nursing 1,* 56–57.

Miller, J. (1983) 'Inspiring Hope.' In J. Miller (ed) *Coping with Chronic Illness – Overcoming Powerlessness.* Philadelphia: F.A. Davies. 287–299.

Miller, J. (1989) 'Hope inspiring strategies of the critically ill.' *Applied Nursing Research 2,* 1 (Feb.), 23–29.

Miller, J. and Wake, M.M. (1992) 'Treating hopelessness: Nursing strategies from six countries.' *Clinical Nursing Research 1,* 4, 347–365.

Morgan, J.P. (1994) 'Bereavement in older adults.' *Journal of Mental Health Counselling 16,* 3, 318–326.

Morse, J.M. and Doberneck, B. (1995) 'Delineating the concept of hope.' *Image 27,* 4, 277–285.

Nightingale, F. (1859) *Notes on Nursing.* Reprinted: Duckworth 1870.

Owen, D. (1989) 'Nurses' perspectives of the meaning of hope in patients with cancer: A qualitative study.' *Oncology Nursing Forum 16,* 1, 75–79.

Parkes, T. (1997) 'Reflections from the outside.' In S. Tilley (ed) *The Mental Health Nurse: Views of Practice and Education.* London: Blackwell Science. 58–72.

Pearlman, L.A. and Saakvatine, K.W. (1995) *Trauma and the Therapist: Countertransference and Vicarious Traumatization in Psychotherapy with Incest Survivors.* London: WW Norton.

Pearson, A. (1992) 'Knowing nursing: Emerging paradigms.' In K. Robinson and B. Vaughan (eds) *Knowledge for Nursing Practice.* London: Butterworth Heinemann.

Peplau, H. (1988) *Interpersonal Relations in Nursing* (2nd edn). New York: G.P. Putnam.

Popper, K. (1965) *Conjectures and Refutations: The Growth of Scientific Knowledge.* New York: Harper and Row.

Raleigh, E.D.H. (1992) 'Sources of hope in chronic illness.' *Oncology Nursing Forum 19*, 3, 443–448.

Raphael, B. (1982) *The Anatomy of Bereavement.* London: Unwin Hyman.

Rawlins, R.P. (1993) 'Hope-hopelessness.' In Rawlins, Williams and Beck (eds) *Mental Health Nursing – A Holistic Life Cycle Approach* (3rd edn). St Louis: Mosby. 257–284.

Ritter, S. (1997) 'Taking stock of psychiatric nursing.' In S. Tilley (ed) *The Mental Health Nurse: Views of Practice and Education.* London: Blackwell Science. 94–117.

Rogers, C. (1952) *Client Centred Therapy: Its Current Practice, Implications and Theory.* London: Constable.

Rogers, C. (1957) 'The necessary and sufficient conditions of therapeutic personality change.' *Consulting Psychology 5*, 2–10.

Rogers, A., Pilgrim, D. and Lacey, R. (1993) *Experiencing Psychiatry: Users' Views of Services.* London: Macmillan/MIND.

Rudman, M.J. (1996) 'User involvement in the nursing curriculum: seeking users' views.' *Journal of Psychiatric and Mental Health Nursing 3*, 195–200.

Sainsbury Centre for Mental Health (1997) *Pulling Together: The Future Roles and Training of Mental Health Staff.* London: Sainsbury Centre for Mental Health.

Sartre, J.P. (1943) in H.J. Blackham (1986) *Six Existentialist Thinkers.* London: Routledge. 58–79.

Schultz, S.E. (1967) *The Phenomenology of the Social World.* North Western University Press.

Shur, R. (1994) *Countertransference Enactment: How Institutions and Therapists Actualize Primitive Internal Worlds.* Northvale: Jason Aronson.

Stapleton, S. (1983) 'Decreasing powerlessness in the chronically ill: A prototype.' In J. Miller (ed) *Coping with Chronic Illness: Overcoming Powerlessness.* Philadelphia: F.A. Davis. 202–220.

Stephenson, C. (1991) 'The concept of hope revisited for nursing.' *Journal of Advanced Nursing 16*, 1456–1461.

Stern, P. (1980) 'Grounded theory methodology: Its uses and applications.' *Image 12*, 11, 20–23.

Stotland, E. (1969) *The Psychology of Hope.* San Francisco: Jossey Bass.

Sullivan, H.S. (1952) *Conceptions of Modern Psychiatry.* Washington DC: William Anderson White Foundation.

Turner, B. (1981) 'Some practical aspects of qualitative data analysis: one way of organising the cognitive processes associated with the generation of grounded theory.' *Quality and Control 15*, 225–245.

Vaillot, M. (1970) 'Hope: The restoration of being.' *American Journal of Nursing*, Feb. 1970.

Worden, J.W. (1988) *Grief Counselling and Grief Therapy.* London: Tavistock/Routledge.

Subject Index

Author Index

About the Author

John Cutcliffe's interest in hope inspiration started in 1993 when working with terminally ill HIV patients and his current research focuses on how nurses care for and inspire hope in suicidal people. Dr Cutcliffe has an extensive track record of research and writing and has produced over 100 peer-reviewed and professional articles. In 2003, he was recognized by the Partnership Group for Science and Engineering as being one of the top twenty young Canadian researchers, and was awarded a Research Leader of Tomorrow citation.